The Life

of the

Meadow Brown

The Life
of the
Meadow Brown

W. H. Dowdeswell

Emeritus Professor of Education,
University of Bath

 HEINEMANN EDUCATIONAL BOOKS

Heinemann Educational Books Ltd
22 Bedford Square, London WC1B 3HH

LONDON EDINBURGH MELBOURNE AUCKLAND
HONG KONG SINGAPORE KUALA LUMPUR NEW DELHI
IBADAN NAIROBI JOHANNESBURG
EXETER (NH) KINGSTON PORT OF SPAIN

© W. H. Dowdeswell 1981

First published 1981

British Library Cataloguing in Publication Data

Dowdeswell, W. H.
  The life of the meadow brown.
  1. Satyridae
  I. Title
  595.78′9   QL561.S3

  ISBN 0-435-60224-1

Printed and bound in Great Britain by
Butler & Tanner Ltd, Frome and London

Contents

Preface *vii*

1 Knowing the meadow brown *1*

2 Beginning an ecological study *20*

3 The mainland stabilizations *43*

4 The meadow brown in Europe *78*

5 Studying island populations *93*

6 The significance of spotting *117*

7 Conclusions and implications *141*

References *156*

Index *161*

Dedication

To Professor E. B. Ford, FRS, with whom I have had the privilege and pleasure of studying the meadow brown for more than forty years.

Preface

This book is about one of the commonest butterflies in Britain which has so far succeeded in eluding the onslaughts on its habitats of modern agriculture and pesticides. It is an insect not only of considerable beauty and natural history interest, but also one which has proved to be particularly suitable for certain kinds of biological investigation.

The material included in the chapters which follow is derived largely from a long series of scientific papers which are summarized in the list of references (p. 156). The main purpose of such publications is to record and evaluate the outcomes of human enquiry rather than to describe the details of the enquiries themselves. This book takes a more intimate look at what went on in practice and how the various stages of the work were planned and implemented. Among other things, it records how, starting from two researchers (Professor E. B. Ford and the author), the numbers involved in the work expanded and the range of research activity spread outside Britain to Italy and Holland.

Much of the time spent in studying the meadow brown has been devoted to unravelling aspects of its life cycle, behaviour, distribution, and variation, few of which have previously been recorded in the literature. Moreover, as so frequently happens when such studies are pursued in depth, many of the existing accounts have proved to be inaccurate. As might be expected in a study of this magnitude, much time and effort have also been expended on problems of experimental design and planning.

The purpose of this book is, as it were, to fill in the background to an extensive piece of biological research. It differs from the usual kind of scientific publication in that the data and the deductions drawn from them are used as a framework into which the background activities of the project are fitted. These relate particularly to the natural history of the meadow brown and the devising and implementation of schemes for studying its ecology. Since the book is based throughout on real situations, I hope it may provide interest and stimulation for future researchers and students of natural history.

While writing this account of our work I have been greatly assisted and encouraged by Professor E. B. Ford, FRS, who has kindly read all the chapters and offered many valuable comments and suggestions. The foundations of our joint studies of the meadow brown were laid on the remote Scottish island of Cara as long ago as 1938, and it is a particular pleasure to be able to place on record the results of our later work and that of our co-workers. Dr Paul Brakefield has read Chapters 3 to 7 and made numerous helpful additions and comments. It has also been a privilege to discuss with him many of the wider aspects of our work on the meadow brown. Dr Valerio Scali has read and commented on Chapter 6 and my thanks are also due to him for his constructive help.

It is a pleasure to express my thanks to Mr S. Beaufoy for his superb photographs (the cover picture of a female meadow brown, and also Plates 1–9 and 14) which illustrate so beautifully a number of butterfly species as adults and also stages in the life cycle of the meadow brown. Dr Valerio Scali kindly provided the originals of Plates 17 and 19 while Mr David Webb took the photographs for Plate 18. I am most grateful to them for their help. The origins of figures, diagrams, and tables are acknowledged, where appropriate, in the text. In this connection, I would particularly like to thank Dr Paul Brakefield for permitting me to use as yet unpublished material from his PhD thesis.

My sincere thanks are also due to Mrs Iris Irving, who prepared the typescript and arranged many of the tables, also to Mrs Elaine Cromwell for typing the Preface and Index.

1981   W. H. Dowdeswell

1

Knowing the meadow
brown

There are two different ways of starting a piece of research in biology or natural history. We can select a plant or animal because of certain attributes it possesses which seem worthy of study. Alternatively, we can first formulate a problem or range of problems and then seek the most suitable organism to assist us in its solution. The second way is undoubtedly the more challenging because the range of decision-making that it demands is likely to be wider and more diversified. It is this approach that we adopted in our studies of the meadow brown.

This book, then, is about a butterfly that we have used to assist us in attempting to answer some fundamental questions in biology. In employing it for this purpose we have had to get to know it intimately and to learn something of its behaviour, life cycle, and the ways in which it has adjusted throughout its range to a great variety of ecological conditions. As we were soon to discover, such information was either not previously obtainable or, when it was, it had all too often been recorded incorrectly.

One of the most important requirements of any piece of biological research is that the organisms used should be easily and unequivocally identifiable by other students who may later wish to make use of the findings. Before proceeding further, therefore, it will be desirable to set the scene, so to speak, by placing the meadow brown and our studies of it in their appropriate context.

Following the pioneer work of Linnaeus and others in the eighteenth century, our Victorian ancestors were much concerned with taxonomy (the determination of classificatory hierarchies) and in particular the criteria used in establishing the binomial system whereby every organism is given two names (usually in Latin), the first denoting its genus and the second its species. The features used in distinguishing one species from another were largely anatomical and this encouraged the accumulation of large collections of preserved specimens illustrating their variation and geographical distribution. Thus in the British Museum (Natural History) and elsewhere collections of butterflies such as the meadow brown are extensive and cover most regions of the insect's range. The majority were accumulated during the early years of this century.

The period following the end of the Second World War heralded significant changes in our approach to the study of living things. Among them was the growing realization that the dependence of organisms on one another and on their physical environment demanded an increased emphasis on the study of ecology. Apart from purely academic considerations, an ecological approach had relevance in such diverse areas as conservation, crop production, and the control of pests. But ecology is not only concerned with the relationships of living organisms as they occur today. It also provides a gateway into the study of their evolution enabling us to determine in varying degree the nature of adaptive change, its rate of occurrence, and some of the factors concerned in bringing it about. This implies the necessity for close ties between ecology, genetics, and mathematics, and the desirability of linking fieldwork with laboratory experimentation. Ecology and ecological genetics are thus near relatives and represent different parts of a spectrum of ecological knowledge. It is against this background of thought that our extensive studies of the meadow brown butterfly have been carried out.

Introducing the meadow brown

The meadow brown is probably the commonest butterfly in Britain. It is an insect of grassy areas such as roadsides, downland, and the edges of cultivated fields. Although a fairly powerful flier, it tends to avoid windswept conditions such as heaths and moorland.

Evidently the widespread abundance of the species has been recognised by entomologists for more than a century. In his book on British Butterflies published in 1837, Sir William Jardine quotes the observations of a Mr Knapp on the meadow brown as follows.

'In these dark and cheerless summers when even the white cabbage butterfly is scarcely to be found, this creature may be seen in every transient gleam, drying its wings and flitting from flower to flower with animation and life, nearly the sole possessor of the field and its sweets. Dry and exhausting as the summer may be, yet this dusky butterfly is uninjured by it, and we see it in profusion hovering about the sapless foliage. In that arid summer of 1826, the abundance of these creatures was so obvious as to be remarked by very indifferent persons.'

The sexes differ from one another in a number of ways (see Plates 1 and 2). The length of the fore-wing in the male (measured from the apex to the point of attachment to the thorax) ranges from 22 mm to 25 mm. The colour of the male on the upper side is almost uniformly dark brown, while on the fore-wing there is a single white-pupilled, apical eyespot (ocellus). Extending outwards from the base of the fore-wing is a conspicuous dark patch of scent-producing scales (androconia) which are absent from the female. The underside of the fore-wing is predominantly orange-brown with the single ocellus much in evidence. The underside of the hind-wing is pale grey to yellow-brown with a basal darker area. Near the margin of the wing and situated in a paler-coloured band is a row of small black spots varying in number from 0 to 5 (Fig. 1). Microscopic evidence shows that these spots are not just patches of the pigment melanin (the pigment which also colours our hair) but are associated with a distinct and localized change in the structure of the scales covering the wings. In contrast to the male, the female appears larger and lighter in colour. The average length of the fore-wing is 2 mm longer than the male and on the upper side there are characteristic orange patches which also appear on the underside. The large eyespot, which is occasionally double, is a feature of both sides. The upper side of the hind-wings is light brown with a conspicuous greyish band while the underside is more brightly coloured than in the male. The row of small black spots tends to be inconspicuous but some spots are frequently present.

The behaviour of the two sexes is quite different. The male gives

a

b

Plate 1 Male meadow brown, (a) wings expanded to show the upper side; (b) wings closed, the two conspicuous black spots on the hind-wing are clearly visible. (× 1.5)

Plate 2 Female meadow brown, (a) wings expanded to show the upper side and the light-coloured patch on the fore-wing; (b) wings closed, insect alert with the large eyespot on the fore-wing showing; (c) wings closed and insect resting with the eyespot on the fore-wing hidden by the hind-wing. Note the absence of spots on the hind-wing—the commonest condition. (× 1.5)

c

the impression of a busy little insect with a wing beat comparatively rapid for its size. Most of its life is spent in replenishing its body fluids from dew and plant juices, and in pursuing freshly emerged females with a view to copulation. The female is a heavier insect and, in addition to the eggs she carries, her body contains a considerable quantity of fat. She is particularly partial to flowers such as knapweed (*Centaurea nigra*) and bramble (*Rubus fruticosus*). Once warmed up she flies powerfully with a weaving motion, the dark upper side and lighter underside alternating and making her difficult to follow against a varied background. Perhaps this behaviour explains the use by Linnaeus of the Latin word *Maniola* (= little ghost) to describe the genus to which the meadow brown belongs. Evidently, he thought the males and females were so different that he grouped them as separate species and so the word

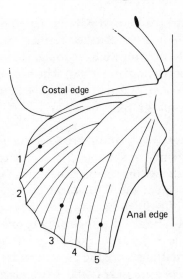

Costal edge

Anal edge

1

2

3

4

5

Figure 1 Diagram of the hind-wing of a meadow brown showing the five possible positions of the spots.

jurtina, which is now used for the species as a whole, was originally applied to the females only.

By day the behaviour of the two sexes is so distinct that they can almost be regarded as separate populations, but in the evening the females usually rejoin the males in the grassy areas where they remain overnight. In Britain, copulation and egg-laying thus tend to occur in the evenings and mornings. As we shall see in Chapter 4, the situation in hot countries such as Italy poses particular problems that have resulted in some remarkable adaptations which will be discussed later. But familiar behaviour patterns in Britain are not necessarily characteristic of temperate climates elsewhere. Charles Lane and Miriam Rothschild have described the activities of the butterfly in a sub-alpine meadow in Austria.[1] When the Sun was temporarily obscured by clouds the meadow browns forsook the grass and flew up into the trees of the surrounding woodlands where they remained until the Sun reappeared, when they returned to the grassland once more. A variation on this theme was observed by the same researchers[2] in Spain in an area near Toledo consisting of open grassland bordering a wood. When chased, the meadow browns darted into the densest part of the wood, settling on the bare earth beneath the trees. Pursued further, they flew up into the trees for shelter. In Britain, we have found that the species avoids woodland (but not woodland rides) which provides an effective barrier to its movement. When disturbed, the butterflies may sometimes fly up into nearby trees but they seldom remain there for long.

A peculiar feature of meadow brown behaviour which makes the butterfly particularly suitable for ecological research is its readiness to fly in almost any weather, including rain. Provided it has had an adequate opportunity to warm up (say half an hour of sunshine) it will either fly of its own accord or can be roused from the vegetation by beating with a stick or dragging along a rope held between two people. Indeed, dull conditions are sometimes the best for sampling populations since the butterflies are relatively easy to catch. On hot days both sexes, and particularly the males, can become extremely agile.

No introduction to the meadow brown would be complete without a brief reference to its familiar scent which will have been experienced in some degree by anyone who has worked extensively with it. As with other odours, such as the smell of tom cats, our sensitivity varies greatly. To some the scent is quite strong, others can only just detect it, while others again are quite unaffected. It has been variously described as reminiscent of an old cigar box, musty hay, and the smell of dirty socks! Professor Ford[3] has pointed out that as far as we know none of the directive odours of female lepidoptera affect the human olfactory sense. Indeed, although female meadow browns may possess the capacity for producing scents detectable by males, we have no knowledge of the extent to which this actually occurs or of the reactions of males to them.

The life cycle of the meadow brown

The scent of the male presumably plays an important part in stimulating the female to pair. The process can last for an hour or more, an essential preliminary being that the female should settle on a firm piece of vegetation such as a rigid grass stem. The male then grips her with his claspers so that the pair are joined end-to-end (Plate 3). If disturbed, they fly clumsily away, the female

Plate 3   Mating in the meadow brown. (× 1.5)

carrying the male who hangs passively. They then settle again elsewhere.

During copulation, the male inserts into the copulation pouch of the female a bag of sperms (spermatophore) which effectively blocks the entrance so that no further pairing is possible. A characteristic behaviour pattern of a female meadow brown when approached by an errant male is a rapid fluttering of wings. This is evidently a signal of rejection and could well be a means of indicating that she has already mated.

A single female in captivity can lay as many as 250 eggs, although the average number is nearer 100. The eggs are deposited on the leaves and stems of grasses. They are cylindrical in shape and ribbed with the surface curving inwards, and flat at the top and bottom (Plate 4). When first laid the egg is a beautiful creamy-white colour speckled with brownish pigment, but as development

Plate 4   Egg of meadow brown butterfly. (× 20)

proceeds it turns a darker purplish brown. Eggs that are unfertilized are identifiable about half way through the developmental period, as their sides appear to sink inwards, becoming concave. The egg stage usually lasts between two and three weeks, the principal factor influencing its duration being temperature.

The larva feeds on a wide variety of grasses, some of its preferences being annual meadow-grass (*Poa annua*) and smooth meadow-grass (*Poa pratensis*). However, it is unable to survive on the coarser species such as purple moor-grass (*Molinia caerulea*) and this may help to explain the low density of the meadow brown populations on acid moors such as Exmoor. During the first part of their life in late summer the caterpillars feed during the daytime. They can be collected by sweeping with a net but extreme care is needed in handling them as they are easily damaged. Once cold weather sets in about November their feeding activities are intermittent and eventually they hibernate, becoming active again in late April. At this stage they are usually about 10 mm long and in their fourth moult (instar). Thereafter, larvae are obtainable until mid-July. When fully grown they are about 25 mm long, bright green, and covered with short, whitish hair (Plate 5). There is a darker green band on the back and also on each side accompanied by a conspicuous whitish-coloured line. A typical feature of the Satyridae (the family to which the meadow brown belongs) is that their caterpillars all have a pair of conspicuous fleshy projections at the hind end. Their relative size and colour varies in the different species, those of the meadow brown being well developed with white tips. Occasionally, the green colour of the caterpillar is replaced by light brown but this variant is rare.

Plate 5 Fully grown caterpillar of the meadow brown in a characteristic feeding position. (× 2)

After hibernation feeding by day ceases and the larvae become nocturnal, no doubt because they provide a tasty meal for insectivorous birds. Sampling larval populations presents obvious problems which need not concern us here but which will be discussed further in the context of laboratory investigations (see Chapter 6). Suffice it to add that a popular misconception perpetuated by textbook writers is that, with the aid of a torch, larvae can be found at night feeding on appropriate species of grasses.[4] Experience of collecting several thousand for breeding purposes has shown this method to be largely impracticable, by far the most effective procedure being to use a sweep net. But even then certain strict rules must be followed if success is to be achieved (see Chapter 6).

The chrysalis (Plate 6) is pale green but darkens as development proceeds. The wing cases are marked with dark brown stripes while the thorax and abdomen are spotted black and brown. The pupa hangs suspended by its anal hooks from a grass stem usually low down among the vegetation. The discarded skin of the caterpillar can be seen attached to its anal extremity (see Plate 6). Again, it is frequently stated[4] that pupae may be found in abundance but practical experience does not support this contention even when the population density is known to be high. The reasons undoubtedly are the excellent camouflage of the pupae and also their tendency (admirably demonstrated in the laboratory) to position themselves much lower in the vegetation than might be supposed from

Plate 6   Chrysalis of the meadow brown in a typical position. (× 2)

the accounts in the textbooks. Indeed, an appreciable proportion actually pupate on the ground. The pupal period normally lasts about three weeks but it may extend to a month in cold weather.

As a result of much experimental work on meadow browns (to be described later) the butterfly can now be bred with ease in captivity, thus enabling us to study its life cycle and gauge its reproductive success with greater precision than would ever have been possible in the field. We will return to these new techniques and their application later on (Chapter 6).

Aspects of classification and geography

The meadow brown belongs to the family Satyridae (the 'browns'), a large group of butterflies comprising nearly a third of the total butterfly fauna inhabiting the warmer parts of Europe. There are eleven British species belonging to eight different genera. The genus to which the meadow brown belongs (*Maniola*) contains the single species, *Maniola jurtina*. Apart from their general inconspicuousness and usually brown colour, there are certain other features that characterize the family, some of which have been mentioned already. Thus the scent scales (androconia) on the fore-wings of the males are usually present in long dark bands. Again, the wings tend to be patterned with spots, some of which are frequently eye-like. Reference has already been made to the spots in the meadow brown (Fig. 1) where as many as five (occasionally six) black dots occur on the outer margin of the hind-wings and a single (occasionally double) pupillated spot is present on each fore-wing. But there are numerous variations on this theme (Plate 7). Thus in the hedge brown (*Pyronia tithonus*, Plate 7a) the black portions of the spots on the underside of the hind-wings are absent, or nearly so, and only their white centres remain. In the ringlet (*Aphantopus hyperanthus*, Plate 7b) large white-pupilled spots occur on both fore- and hind-wings. In the speckled wood (*Pararge aegeria*, Plate 7c) the black element of the spots on the hind-wings occurs on the upper side only; while in the marbled white (*Melanargia galathea*, Plate 7d), in spite of its aberrant colouration, spotting is much in evidence on the undersides of both the fore- and hind-wings.

The family Satyridae is also characterized by certain features in the young stages. Thus Professor Ford[3] describes the eggs as generally grooved and melon-shaped. The larvae, like those of the meadow brown described earlier, are covered with downy hairs and do not have spines but all have a pair of anal projections. They are grass feeders. The pupae, like those of the meadow brown, are usually suspended head downwards from plants by their tail-hooks (Plate 6) but can also lie in or on the ground either in a cocoon or without one.

The meadow brown (*Maniola jurtina*) is the predominant member of the genus in Europe, the only other species being the Sardinian meadow brown (*Maniola nurag*) found exclusively on the

a

b

Plate 7 Some variations in spot patterns among British Satyridae ('browns'). All the photographs are of undersides: (a) hedge brown (*Pyronia tithonus*), (b) ringlet (*Aphantopus hyperanthus*), (× 1.5) (c) speckled wood (*Pararge aegeria*), (d) marbled white (*Melanargia galathea*), (× 1.5).

island of Sardinia. Moving further east we find M. *cypricola* confined to Cyprus, and a West Asian form, M. *telmessia*. All these other species exhibit the five-spot motif on the underside of the hind-wings so characteristic of M. *jurtina*. It is thus a significant fact that the incidence of spotting has overriden the evolution of species in *Maniola*.[5] All Satyrine butterflies bear evidence of the action of hereditary systems which, as far as spot patterns are concerned, produce comparable results. Indeed, this peculiar form of marking extends beyond the family Satyridae into others (Plate 8) such as the Nymphalidae which includes our marsh fritillary (*Euphydryas aurinia*), the Lycaenidae typified by the black hairstreak (*Strymonidia pruni*) and the Vanessidae exemplified by the painted lady (*Vanessa cardui*). This widespread occurrence of spotting in several different families suggests that the gene systems controlling it must be of great antiquity.

The meadow brown also forms a number of distinct geographical sub-species throughout its range which are recognized by

a

Plate 8   The spotting motif in families other than the Satyridae, (a) the Nymphalidae—marsh fritillary (*Euphydryas aurinia*), (× 2) (b) the Lycaenidae—black hairstreak (*Strymonidia pruni*), (× 1.5) (c) the Vanessidae—painted lady (*Vanessa cardui*), (× 2).

b

c

variations in size, colour, and reproductive anatomy.[6] We need be concerned here only with the three occurring in the British Isles. The most widespread is the sub-species *splendida* which, as its name implies, is a more striking butterfly than the usual form of the meadow brown. Its distribution is confined to western Scotland from just north of Glasgow to Sutherland, and it is also found on a number of the western islands. On the wing the butterfly gives the impression of being larger and brighter than usual due to the increase in orange colouration in both sexes. Thus the male has an orange patch on the upper and underside of the fore-wings, while in the female the orange marking has extended on the fore-wings and invaded the hind-wings as well. The sub-species *iernes* is found only in Ireland and in its colouration shows tendencies in the direction of *splendida*, but in lesser degree. In the Isles of Scilly the meadow brown forms a further sub-species known as *cassiteridum*. In some respects this resembles *iernes* but the insects are slightly larger, particularly the females. The most obvious distinguishing feature is the underside of the hind-wings which, instead of presenting uniform areas of different shades of brown, is characteristically mottled. In all three sub-species the single eyespot on the fore-wings and the variable five-spot pattern on the hind-wings remain unchanged.

Methods of study

The point was made earlier that there is much to be said for viewing biological research as a problem-solving operation in which the selection of an organism or range of organisms for study is a secondary rather than a primary consideration. Thus, in an ecological context, we might ask the question 'Is there a difference in the survival rates of individual insects belonging to small and large populations?' To answer such a question two of the attributes of a suitable species would have to be a readiness to form populations of different density and an ease of sampling. In addition, other features of a more personal kind might have to be taken into consideration. These could include the experience and background knowledge of the researchers, and financial aspects which could be significant if an otherwise suitable species was located in an out-of-the-way habitat. In pursuing such a quest perfection is never achieved. Living material which may prove highly favourable for some purposes can be a disaster for others. Moreover, it is quite likely that requirements may change as experience increases and new avenues open up as a result of increasing knowledge. Some of the advantages and disadvantages of a particular species may thus remain undetected until the work is well advanced.

As later chapters will show, this is precisely the situation we have encountered when working with the meadow brown. To its credit, it should be added that in spite of our increasing and varied demands upon it, the balance of suitability has remained over-whelmingly on its side.

2

Beginning an ecological study

The fact that plants and animals can vary, and their ability to transmit beneficial variations from one generation to the next, provide the basis for their adaptation to differing ecological conditions and the foundation for evolutionary change. For such reasons, Professor E. B. Ford and I have for long been interested in problems relating to variation; indeed, our studies in this field have now covered a span of more than forty years. When planning our research in the early days, some typical questions we asked ourselves were, 'What is the extent of a particular variant in terms of its magnitude and distribution?' 'To what degree is it inherited and how?' 'How are its effects manifested in populations of different sizes?' 'How can population size in mobile species be determined?' 'Can we detect the effects of selection in promoting evolutionary adjustments?'

One of the main difficulties with this sort of work is that observable changes in wild populations frequently take place rather slowly so that considerable periods of time may be needed in order to assess them fully and draw reliable conclusions from them. However, as we shall see later, modern sampling and mathematical techniques, combined with an increased knowledge of the mechanism of evolution, have enabled us to obtain worthwhile results in a matter of only a few generations.

One of the earliest examples of prolonged study of an animal population was that of H. D. and E. B. Ford[7] on a colony of the marsh fritillary butterfly (*Euphydryas aurinia*) which extended over a period of nineteen years, although previous records covering a further thirty-six years gave a total coverage of fifty-five years. Over this span of time the fortunes of the colony passed through several phases. From 1881 until 1897 was a period of abundance, but from then onwards numbers began to decline until by 1920 the insect was regarded as rare. But the four years 1921–4 heralded a great increase in the population once more, which thereafter stabilized until the end of the observations in 1935, by which time a slight tendency to decrease was observable. From 1881–1920 the appearance of the butterflies, judged by their wing pattern and size, was relatively stable. But as numbers increased from 1921–4, so too did the amount of variation, hardly two individuals being alike. Ford[7] records that degrees of variation were closely correlated with the incidence of deformities, the more extreme departures from normality being clumsy when flying or even unable to fly at all. From 1925 onwards variation declined. However, the form now occurring differed appreciably from that which had characterized the colony during the 1881–1920 period. Evidently, the outburst in numbers and the increased variation associated with it had provided the butterfly with an opportunity for evolution, which it had taken.

This series of observations, carried out long before modern experimental methods had been developed, illustrates beautifully how the careful and systematic study of wild populations in the field can lead to findings of fundamental ecological and evolutionary interest. To the best of my knowledge, this important lead has never been taken up using present-day methods, either in this species or any other. The work certainly needs to be repeated in a modern context.

For the study of wild populations, one of the most important requirements is a measure of isolation. This ensures that any changes observed are taking place within the population and are not influenced by the effects of immigration or emigration. Ecological barriers to movement are of many kinds. As far as the meadow brown is concerned woodland exerts a powerful effect in restricting flight, as was mentioned in Chapter 1. But a more effective barrier still is the sea. Islands, therefore, by virtue of their isolation, can be regarded as outdoor laboratories, and it is for this reason that much of our work on ecology and ecological genetics has been carried out in an island context.

Judging significance

Mention was made in the previous section of the evolution of modern experimental techniques for the study of ecology. Some of the most powerful of these have been in the area of mathematics where a variety of statistical methods now enable us to compare sets of related results and to determine the degree of significance of any differences between them. There is no such thing as 'absolute significance' (i.e. certainty) where such comparisons are concerned. All we can do is to determine the probability (P) on some hypothesis, that a particular situation will occur. In calculating probabilities from the wide range of results included in the chapters that follow, a variety of statistical methods have been employed, by far the commonest being the chi-squared (χ^2) test. Description of the arithmetic procedures involved is outside the scope of this book, but they can be obtained from one of the many introductions to statistics now available.

The difference between two comparable sets of data is said to be significant if the probability of its occurrence by chance equals or is less than 1 in 20 (i.e. $P = 0.05$ or less). The reason for choosing this apparently arbitrary criterion of significance is that a chance of 1 in 20 stands on the normal probability curve at a point where it starts to become very steep. Thus, a figure for P of only slightly less than 0.05 indicates that the chance of obtaining such a result by luck is, in fact, quite remote.

Just as statistical techniques such as chi-squared can be used to judge difference, so they can be employed to assess similarity. This is important in determining whether or not there is justification for adding two or more comparable sets of results together for comparison with other data. Thus $P > 0.05$ indicates homogeneity and that accumulation is therefore justified, whereas $P < 0.05$ is evidence of heterogeneity.

Studies on the island of Cara

Our first attempt at studying variation quantitatively took place on Cara, a small uninhabited island 1.5 km long and 0.8 km wide. It is situated about 1.5 km south of the island of Gigha and 5.5 km west of Tayinloan on the mainland of the Mull of Kintyre in south-west Scotland. Among its characteristics were a wide diversity of vegetation, a total absence of trees and a summer climate that was alternately very hot and raining (mostly the latter). Another endearing feature of the island was the local spirit, the brownie, whose main preoccupation, according to the inhabitants of nearby Gigha, was maintaining the interests of the owners, the Macdonalds, against those of the neighbouring Campbells to the north. That it took a lively interest in our presence was amply evidenced by the strange goings-on at night which we were never able to explain.

The purpose of a fortnight's visit was to find a species of butterfly or moth which could provide the basis for a local study of variation that we hoped might be extended more widely later on. A second intention was to use the selected species to try out a method of estimating its population numbers by marking, releasing, and recapturing. The detailed application of this technique will be described fully later in this chapter. However, the principle on which it is based is extremely simple. Suppose we are studying a population of butterflies and we catch say 50 specimens and mark them by some method so that they can readily be identified. We then release them into the population and allow them time to assort at random (in say 24 hours). After the marked and unmarked specimens have thoroughly mixed, a further 45 insects are captured. Among them are found 10 bearing the previous day's marks. We can then calculate the *flying* population as $(50 \times 45)/10 = 225$.

For such work we needed an insect which was variable, common, easy to capture, convenient to mark, and which randomized readily when released. None of the ten species of butterflies occurring on Cara met these requirements and we eventually selected a night-flying moth, the dark arches (*Apamea monoglypha*). This had the advantage of variability, its colour ranging from melanic (black) to pale brown, also of size and abundance. Its great disadvantage was the necessity of collecting it at night. An added complication was the fact, already mentioned, that the island supported no trees. In order to collect the moths at night it was therefore necessary either to use a light trap (which we did not possess) or to paint a treacle mixture on suitable surfaces as an attractant. As far as we were concerned, such collecting surfaces had to be prepared from pieces of drift-wood collected on the shore.

Although the marking of insects with cellulose paint and felt pens is now commonplace, it must be remembered that at the time of the work on Cara in 1937 no-one had yet attempted to mark butterflies and moths. Such marking as was carried out by naturalists was confined exclusively to the ringing of birds and this solely for the purpose of studying their movement. Our first attempt at marking the wings of the dark arches was by means of a ticket punch which clipped a small hole near the margin of the fore-wing. The position of the hole could be used as a rough date mark thereby providing a way of identifying multiple recaptures. The ticket punch technique was open to the obvious objection that it inflicted damage on the insect and we were well aware that if we continued to use it we would have somehow to estimate the possible influence of marking on a moth's expectation of life. In the event this was to prove unnecessary as more effective methods of marking became available soon afterwards.

Aided by Professor R. A. Fisher, the analysis of our results showed that the population of dark arches moths on Cara during our visit (17 July to 1 August) was approximately 4500, the maximum number flying on any one night being about 1000.[8] The daily elimination rate in the population was roughly 50 per cent but how much of this was attributable to our marking methods we shall never know. In carrying out research work the unexpected sometimes happens and it is always wise to be vigilant. Thus, on visiting our treacled planks, which we had propped up against rocks near the ground after dark, we were surprised to find the wings of moths, including those of dark arches, lying nearby which had evidently been dismembered from their bodies. Observation showed that the resting moths were providing a welcome source of food for the local rat population and appropriate action was needed to place the boards out of the reach of such predators.

The quantification of colour variation in the dark arches is also interesting as it represents one of the earliest attempts at this sort of measurement. Since the gradation from black to almost white is continuous we were able to establish eight grades exemplified by specimens which we kept for colour comparisons. The data from samples of 333 males and 313 females are summarized in Fig. 2. A statistical test shows the two sets of data to be significantly different from one another ($P < 0.01$). The interest of this finding lies not so

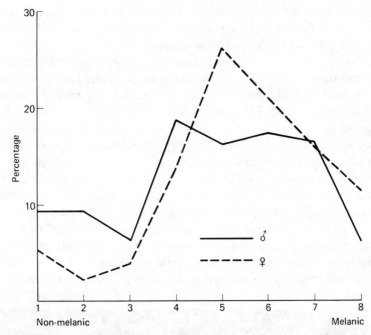

Figure 2 Colour variation in the dark arches moth (*Apamea monoglypha*) on Cara Island.

much in the light it throws on the range of colour variation in the dark arches, as in the fact that the pattern of variation is evidently different in the two sexes. As we shall see later, this is a situation that we have also encountered in the meadow brown.

Early studies on the island of Tean

Three years' experience of conditions on Cara convinced us of the need to transfer our studies elsewhere. The necessity for working at night proved a very inefficient use of our limited time and the systematic study of day-flying species such as butterflies was precluded by the uncertain weather. In the strong winds and driving rain the whole of the butterfly population was frequently grounded for days on end. Accordingly, we changed our location to the Isles of Scilly and camped on the uninhabited island of Tean situated at its nearest point about 300 m west of the large island of St Martin's.

Tean is approximately 0.8 km long and 0.4 km wide at its broadest part. The climate and the nature of the terrain proved to be ideal for the kind of work we had attempted earlier.

Our extensive work in the Scillies and the relationship of the distribution of butterflies with the ecology of the islands will be considered shortly. Suffice it to say here that our first arrival on Tean on 23 August 1938 soon showed that our choice of butterfly species for study was limited to two, the meadow brown (*Maniola jurtina*) and the common blue (*Polyommatus icarus*). Both appeared to occur in abundance. But although the female meadow browns were still fresh and common, the males were already worn and scarce, indicating that the emergence was well advanced. By contrast both sexes of the common blue were fresh and the emergence was evidently still in progress. We therefore decided to study the common blue as we were particularly concerned to find if marking, release, and recapture could be carried out on so small an insect (Plate 9). As subsequent experience showed, this was an

Plate 9   Common blue (*Polyommatus icarus*) at rest. The pattern of spotting on the underside of both wings is more complex than that of the meadow brown. (× 2.5)

unfortunate choice although it seemed the obvious one at the time; for the common blue proved to have two serious drawbacks. First, it was slow to appear on the wing in the morning and this restricted the time available for sampling the population, since at least an hour of sunshine was necessary before the butterflies were prepared to fly. It also meant that for the estimation of numbers by the mark, release, and recapture method, animals marked the previous day and released into the population in the evening needed several hours before their distribution was fully randomized. A second problem derived from the fact that the common blue will only fly in sunshine. Once settled during a dull or cool spell it might take a considerable time before it was warmed sufficiently to fly again. Moreover, while inactive, no amount of beating the vegetation will rouse it.

But in spite of these drawbacks we were able to carry out a considerable programme involving the estimation of numbers of common blues on Tean using the method already applied to the dark arches moth on Cara. Our experience there had highlighted the limitations of the ticket punch as a means of marking the wings of butterflies and moths. These were largely overcome by the use of dots of quickly drying cellulose paints, a technique to which our attention had been directed in time to try out the new method on Tean. This procedure, now largely superseded by felt-tipped pens, was a success for several reasons. Most important, its application to the wings of butterflies involved no damage, either by piercing of the wing membrane or by removing scales prior to its application. Indeed, there was even evidence that it might improve the performance of ageing specimens by sealing some of the remaining scales into the wing membrane.

The paint's rapid drying properties ensured that coloured dots did not remain liquid for long, thereby reducing the likelihood of smudging or of the wings sticking together. Again, the paint was available in a variety of colours and use of these provided a means of greatly increasing the amount of information that a butterfly's wings could carry. Appropriate codes based on the colours and positions of paint marks enabled us not only to identify multiple recaptures and the dates when they were previously caught but also the locality where they were captured. Aided thus, and also by the vastly improved weather conditions compared with the west coast of Scotland, we were able to subject our method for the estimation of numbers to a much more exhaustive test.

The eventual procedure adopted will be discussed further in the context of work on the meadow brown. All that need be said here is that we were able to estimate the population of common blues on Tean over a period of nine days during which it ranged from about 350 at the beginning to almost nothing at the end.[9] It was also possible to show that over the period from 26 August to 8 September 450–500 common blues died including about 100 which emerged during that period.

Two important assumptions on which such work rests are that insect movement within the sampling area is at random and that the island population is isolated, thus precluding significant immigration or emigration. To test the first hypothesis we checked, over a period of several days, the distribution of marked specimens that had supposedly randomized by recording the number of individuals captured upwind and downwind of the point of release after marking. The results turned out to be essentially similar in each direction. The nearest island (St Martin's), which also supported a large population of common blues, was about 300 m to the east at the nearest point. If migration were in fact taking place, this seemed to be the most likely crossing place. Accordingly, as the numbers of marked blues built up on Tean we started collecting on the neighbouring shore as well. By the last day, the number marked on Tean had reached 195 and the total caught in the area opposite over a period of five days was 176—all of them unmarked.

Variation in the common blue

Our other studies of the common blue concerned its variation and were essentially a continuation of the work we had begun on Cara with the dark arches. The species has a wide distribution extending throughout Europe, temperate Asia, and North Africa. However, it does not occur in North America, so the Isles of Scilly and the west coast of Ireland represent its westerly limits. Now, as an animal or plant nears the limit of its range we might expect it to be under increasing pressure in attempting to adapt to a variety of ecological environments some of which could be rather unsuitable for it. Thus, if the species is variable, as in the common blue, we should look for evidence of increasing variation in populations as they extend westwards. The pattern on the underside of the fore- and hind-wings of the common blue consists of a greyish background covered with numerous small black dots (Plate 9) which bear no resemblance to those of the meadow brown (Plate 1b). Sometimes certain of these are absent or reduced; sometimes they are enlarged and may run together to form bars. Most of these varieties have been given names which need not concern us here.

Our attempt to study this range of variation consisted of applying an arbitrary score to each variant depending on its apparent magnitude (evaluation). Dividing this by the number in the sample gave a variation index. The scheme proved to be too crude for formal statistical analysis but, nonetheless, the limited results are sufficiently indicative to be worth recording. We sampled populations in Tiverton (Devon), Hayle (Cornwall), St Martin's (Scilly), and Tean (Scilly). The results are summarized in Table 1.

Table 1 Variation of the common blue (*Polyommatus icarus*) in the south-west of England.

	Locality							
	Tiverton (Devon)		Hayle (Cornwall)		St Martin's (Scilly)		Tean (Scilly)	
	M	*F*	*M*	*F*	*M*	*F*	*M*	*F*
Sample	31	5	58	50	52	50	52	53
Variation evaluation	8	0	23	19	57	43	52	44
Variation index	0.26	0	0.40	0.38	1.10	0.86	1.0	0.83

The figures for the variation index suggest that the male may be the more variable of the two sexes but larger samples would be needed to establish this view. However, there is a much stronger indication of increased variation in both sexes towards the limits of the species' range. As we shall see, these findings accord closely with those for the meadow brown whose world-wide distribution is somewhat similar to that of the common blue.

Numbers in meadow brown populations

Our pioneer studies of the use of the mark, release, and recapture method for estimating the numbers of the common blue on Tean were successful both in determining population size and in establishing a method for calculating rates of survival. Nonetheless it was clear that for population studies of this kind the meadow brown was infinitely preferable. Its larger size greatly facilitated handling, the avoidance of damage in marking, and the use of a more elaborate colour code for recording information (as many as six paint marks are possible on each hind-wing). Its abundance eased problems of sampling; but above all, its readiness to fly in almost any weather permitted a far more efficient use of our limited time both in collecting and in ensuring the rapid randomization of marked specimens once released. Accordingly, we decided to repeat the work on the common blue using the meadow brown instead.

Earlier in the chapter mention was made of the principle employed in estimating the size of a population of flying insects by the method of mark, release, and recapture. As a result of our work on the common blue the scheme had become considerably elaborated and a brief description of it is now needed. As we saw earlier (p. 23), the basic procedure is as follows. A sample of say 100 insects (S_1) in a population is captured, marked, and released, and then allowed to randomize within the population from which it was withdrawn. When randomization is complete (say a day later) a further sample (S_2) is captured which may contain a few individuals (R_1) marked the previous day. The total flying population can then be calculated as $(S_1 \times S_2)/R_1$. The process can be continued for as long as required; the greater the number of samples, the more precise will the estimate of population density become. The record of a period of sampling can conveniently be summarized in the form of a triangular trellis. Figure 3 shows some typical results obtained for one of the colonies of the meadow brown on Tean. The dates of the samples run horizontally along the top of the diagram. From the position of each date, lines run downwards to the left and to the right at 45 degrees so as to intersect. The total daily samples are entered at the end of the column running down to the left from the date in question, while the total butterflies released are included at the end of the corresponding column

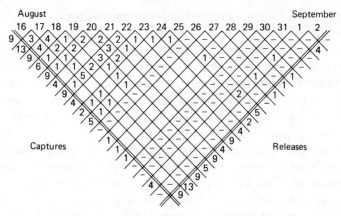

Figure 3 Results tabulated as a trellis in the capture–mark–recapture method of estimating numbers in meadow brown populations.

running down to the right. In the event of there being no recaptures on a particular day, these two numbers will, of course, be the same, except on occasions (rare in the meadow brown) when an insect is damaged in marking and has to be killed. All recoveries are shown in the body of the table and the number of marks they carry, together with those of insects marked for the first time, represent the total 'marks released'. With this method it is not necessary to collect a sample every day. In the table a dash (-) shows that no recaptures were possible on a particular date, either because no insects were caught or because none were released the day before.

A few examples will make this method of presentation clear. In Fig. 3 at the extreme top left of the table and below the date 16 August is the number 9 at the head of the 'Captures' column. A corresponding figure appears under 'Releases' showing that on that date the whole sample was successfully marked for the first time and liberated. On the next day 13 butterflies were caught, among them 3 captured the day before, each bearing a single mark. These appear on the table in the square to the left of the appropriate date. The total number of insects released was also 13 and this figure appears at the end of the column corresponding to 17 August. The entries for 26 August are all dashes, showing there was no collecting on that day and therefore no recaptures.

Simple direct estimates of the daily flying population can be made from the table. For example, consider the line running down to the right from 17 August: out of 9, 6, 9, 4, 9, 4, 2, 5 (total 48) meadow browns caught from 18–25 August, 4, 2, 1, 1, 5, 1, 1 (total 15) recaptures belonged to the 13 marked on 17 August. Thus the total number flying on that date can be calculated as approximately $(48 \times 13)/15 = 41$ insects. But in populations of animals numbers do not remain constant for long. Among butterflies, immigration and the emergence of new individuals will tend to increase them while emigration and deaths have the opposite effect. In studies of any duration, therefore, the influence of these factors must be taken into account. This is done by comparing the number of recaptures *expected* in a population distributed at random with those actually *obtained*, using as a basis for the calculation the number of marks existing from day to day. It would be inappropriate to pursue the analysis further here but anyone interested can easily obtain the information from a relevant publication.[10]

The meadow brown on Tean

Our study of the common blue on Tean had shown that the island could be divided into a number of distinct ecological zones, some

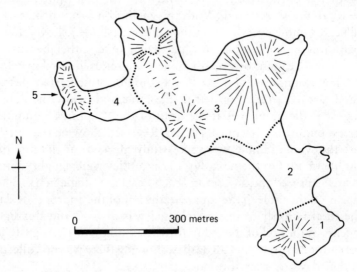

Figure 4   Map of Tean (Isles of Scilly).

of which were populated by the butterfly while others were either isolated by effective barriers or covered by vegetation which prevented colonization by that species. The meadow brown proved to be similarly localized in its distribution.[11] The island could conveniently be divided into five areas (see Fig. 4). Of these, Areas 1, 3, and 5 were colonized by the butterfly while Areas 2 and 4 were not. Area 1 comprised about one-third of the southern limb of the island terminating in a small hill about 15 m high, mostly covered by bracken, bramble, and gorse. Interspersed with this were patches

Plate 10 Southerly view of Tean (Isles of Scilly). Areas 1 and 2 viewed from Area 3. The large island in the distance is St Mary's.

of long grass of various species, which were the favourite habitats of the meadow brown. Area 2 constituted the remainder of the southern limb of the island; it was windswept, the growth of grass was stunted and it was not colonized by meadow browns, but formed an effective barrier between Area 1 and Area 3 further north (Plate 10). Area 3 constituted the main body of the island and included three small hills of which the highest was about 40 m. The predominant vegetation was bracken, bramble, and gorse, but there were also considerable areas of grass which supported the main population of butterflies. Area 4 to the west was so windswept and eroded that it presented an almost lawn-like appearance (Plate 11). Area 5 was a small isolated promontory at the extremity of the western limb, consisting of a mound about 9 m high with small

Plate 11   Westerly view of the west limb of Tean (Isles of Scilly). The closely cropped grass in the foreground is Area 4. To the far left is Area 5 and on the right is Area 3. The island in the distance is St Helen's.

patches of bracken and long grass, and a few stunted brambles (Plate 11).

The distribution of the meadow brown on Tean thus presented a compact ecological picture: a relatively large central massif (Area 3), heavily populated and separated by barriers (Areas 2 and 4) from two much smaller regions, both supporting populations of proportionate size. One of these (Area 1) was situated at the southern, and the other (Area 5), the smallest of all, at the western extremity of the island.

The three populations were sampled for a period of 18 days, a releasing point being established in each area, more or less in the middle, from which the marked butterflies were liberated each evening. As might be imagined, the numbers of the three populations differed greatly. Using the capture–mark–recapture technique outlined earlier, we concluded that the maximum numbers flying in Area 1 were about 1400; in Area 3 were roughly 7000; and in Area 5 they were 250 or less.

Mention was made earlier of the value to be gained from a comparison of the recaptures expected in a population with those actually obtained, using as a basis for computation the number of marks existing from day to day. The results of dividing observed by expected survival rates expressed as a percentage are summarized in Table 2.

Table 2 Comparison of observed and expected survival in the meadow brown on Tean expressed as a percentage.

Area	Males (%)	Females (%)
1	107.3	108.2
3	104.7	64.6
5	89.6	74.3

Particularly revealing is a comparison of survival in the two small populations in Areas 1 and 5. Area 1 was approximately 150 m by 120 m and harboured 1400 individuals at a maximum, while Area 5 was about 140 m by 60 m with a maximum population of less than 250. Thus, while the density of meadow browns in Area 1 was $0.08/m^2$, that in Area 5 was only $0.03/m^2$. The difference in the survival rates of the butterflies in the two areas could be explained partly in terms of the more favourable conditions prevailing in Area 1 both for food and shelter. Area 5 was more remote, sparse, and windswept; but above all, it was considerably smaller. This means that a higher proportion of its population will have tended to be in the vicinity of the perimeter at any one time and hence will have stood a good chance of straying and becoming lost, or of being blown away by the high winds. Hence we would have expected the level of survival to be lower in Area 5 than in Area 1. The results confirmed our expectation. The estimate of survival rate of females in Area 3 is something of an anomaly which can probably be attributed to the inadequate sampling of a large population and therefore insufficient recaptures.

As in our studies of the common blue, the estimation of numbers and survival in the meadow brown rested on the assumption that we were dealing with isolated populations. Thus it was important to determine not only whether immigration and emigration were taking place between Tean and the neighbouring island of St Martin's, but also the extent, if at all, to which leakage was occurring on the island itself between one area and another. As explained earlier, the channel between Tean and St Martin's to the east is only about 300 m wide at the nearest point (Plate 12). During our stay on Tean we released 1003 marked specimens (excluding recaptures), none of which was found on our frequent visits to St

Plate 12 St Martin's (Isles of Scilly) viewed from the nearest point on Tean. The 300 metres of sea provide a barrier to meadow brown movement.

Martin's. On 26 August we captured another 48 meadow browns and having given them a distinguishing mark released them on St Martin's at the point nearest to Tean. None was caught on Tean during the remaining 7 days of our stay. There was, therefore, reasonable evidence that migration by butterflies across the causeway from one island to the other is a rare event.

The populations inhabiting the three areas on Tean proved to be subject to a high degree of ecological isolation, which is remarkable considering the flying capacity of the meadow brown. Thus, during a stay of 15 days we recaught 183 marked specimens. Of this total, only three were recaptured in an area different from that in which they had previously been caught. This not only upheld the view that the three areas supported discrete ecological communities, but also the wider contention that some butterfly species are far less mobile than their structure might suggest. Even quite minor barriers such as 100 m of windswept ground can evidently constitute an almost total barrier to movement in the meadow brown.

While working in Scilly, Professor Ford and I made an extraordinary observation one evening with a bearing not only on the local movement of meadow browns but also on the wider issue of butterfly migration in general, and it is appropriate to include it here. We had been out mackerel fishing and were about to drop anchor at roughly 1900 GMT on 30 August when a small white butterfly (*Pieris rapae*) flew weakly across the boat and alighted on the water, which was dead calm, with its wings outstretched. About two minutes later it made one or two convulsive movements, and to our astonishment, succeeded in rising. It flew about 10 m and settled again, once more with wings outspread, only to repeat the performance a few minutes afterwards. The evening was already cool and dusk was falling and, since the butterfly appeared unable to rise again, we rescued it with a boat-hook. There seems little doubt that in warm daytime conditions and a calm sea the butterfly would have been quite capable of continuing its journey. Strangely, this observation, although duly published,[12] does not seem to have featured in any of the accounts of insect migration. Yet its significance could be considerable in helping to account for the remarkable migratory feats of some butterflies like the milkweed (*Danaus plexippus*), reputed to cross the Atlantic, as well as contributing to localized movements of species such as the meadow brown within an archipelago like the Isles of Scilly. The chances of anyone observing a butterfly resting on the sea are indeed remote.

Spotting as an index of variation

The sampling of butterfly populations is best done by catching the insects in a net and then transferring them to pill boxes, one to a box. For a meadow brown, the size of box needs to be about 50 mm × 40 mm. Provided the boxes are kept in the shade the butterflies will remain quiet and undamaged for several hours. The most convenient time for marking is when the insects are least active in the late afternoon or evening. This minimizes the time spent in removing the animals from the pill boxes. Provided a butterfly is resting, this operation is comparatively easy, the insect being held between the fingers or with a pair of entomological forceps (we prefer the latter) with its wings closed. But in spite of all precautions a few insects will become active at the critical moment and manage to escape. For this reason it is important that marking operations be carried out in a tent with the flaps closed and with a net instantly handy. Experience has shown that the most efficient division of labour is for one person to be responsible for handling the butterflies, extracting them from the pill boxes, holding them still for marking, assessing recapture and other data, and returning them to the boxes when marked; while the other does the marking and recording.

On Tean the meadow browns were either released immediately after marking or, if it was too late for them to fly, the next morning when they were fully warmed up. On the evening of 16 August 1946, Professor Ford and I were marking the day's samples when we noticed that the number of spots on the hind-wings (see Chapter 1) appeared to vary from one insect to another. Now variation in an animal or plant, no matter how trivial it appears to be, is always potentially interesting as it may be indicative of the adaptation of the population in which it occurs to a particular set of ecological conditions. It is doubly interesting if, as appeared to be the situation with spotting, the variant can be easily quantified. We therefore decided to score all subsequent samples for spotting as well as for paint marks. This necessitated the development of a standardized scoring technique so that results obtained at different times and in differing contexts would be comparable. The procedure we devised and which we have never found it necessary to alter, was as follows. As was explained earlier, the spots are situated in definite positions on the underside of the hind-wings (see Fig. 1, p. 7) and vary in number from 0 to 5 (very occasionally 6 are present). Usually they are symmetrical on the two wings but occasionally they vary by one spot or sometimes more. For consistent scoring it was important to discover whether such variation was random or whether there was a consistent bias in favour of one side rather than the other. Examination of large samples involving many hundreds of meadow browns showed that spot-variation was indeed random in both sexes. We therefore made the arbitrary decision always to score the left side only. In some regions, such as the Isles of Scilly, the butterflies have a powdering of blackish scales on the underside of the hind-wings which also occurs in lesser degree on individuals elsewhere. A spot was regarded as absent if it could not be distinguished from a black scale which might have occurred anywhere on the wing. We found that the process of scoring was best carried out by two people, one examining the butterflies and the other recording the results. It was important that the two worked independently of each other so that the one doing the scoring of spot-values was not aware of the accumulating frequency distribution

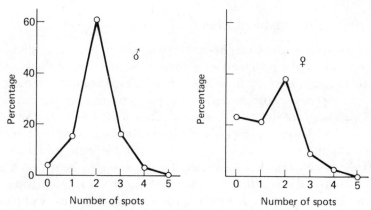

Figure 5 Spot-distribution of the meadow brown on Tean (Isles of Scilly) in 1946.

recorded by the other, lest unconscious bias might influence his decisions.

The results of our first samples scored in this way[11, 13] are shown graphically in Fig. 5. Two comments need to be made about them. Statistical analysis showed that spotting in the three areas was similar and had evidently not been affected by their degree of isolation from one another (for the males the statistical similarity is overwhelming; for the females $P < 0.5$). More remarkable was the difference in the spot patterns of the two sexes: in the males the distribution was approximately symmetrical, with a maximum at 2 spots; in the female it was bimodal with the smaller mode at 0 and the larger at 2 spots. As we had found in the common blue, the two sexes evidently differed in their variability, but whereas in the blue the male appeared to be the more variable, in the meadow brown it was the female.

These unexpected and exciting findings on Tean raised many questions. What was the spot-distribution of mainland populations of the meadow brown? Were distributions stabilized or did they fluctuate from year to year? What evidence was there that spotting had adaptive significance as an indicator that the insect was adjusting to varying ecological conditions? Our attempts to obtain answers to these questions and others deriving from them will be the subject of later chapters.

Living on uninhabited islands

Much has been said so far about our work on uninhabited islands, but what of the problems of human existence under these and similar conditions? By now it will be clear that in order to carry out studies of the sort outlined in the previous pages it will usually be necessary to live on the spot. Uninhabited islands can be somewhat desolate places, particularly when the weather is bad, so it is important to come prepared. One of the main problems is dividing one's time between scientific and domestic activities; it is all too easy, if due care is not exercised, for the latter to predominate. The periodic acquisition of provisions, for instance, can consume an inordinate amount of time and the guiding principle should therefore be to aim at the greatest degree of self-sufficiency possible. The additional baggage necessary to achieve this will prove in the long run to have been well worthwhile. A major deficiency on uninhabited islands can be a reliable supply of water. On Cara there was a spring which bubbled up through the ground into a muddy area colonized by a dense growth of rushes and used by the local rat and duck population as a bathing place. All water had first to be filtered through a piece of muslin or allowed to sediment in order to remove the suspended particles of peat, and then boiled or sterilized with water tablets. On Tean there was an ancient pump used as a water source for cattle, but the water tasted so nasty and contained so much suspended matter as to make it undrinkable. It was therefore necessary to obtain all our water from the neighbouring island of St Martin's. For such purposes, and in case of an unexpected emergency, it is essential to have one's own means of communication and not to rely solely on others, however near they may seem to be. Our transport was a small rowing boat which we hired and which served our purpose admirably. We found it was generally necessary to make an evening visit to St Martin's, the nearby inhabited island, on alternate days.

For an expedition of two people such as ours, two tents are essential, one used for sleeping and the temporary storage of light equipment during daytime, the other for stores, cooking, and for use as a work tent. Islands tend to be windswept and treeless, so the siting of a camp can be vital. Plate 13 shows a typical site on Tean with the tents pitched in the lee of the small hill in Area 1

Plate 13 Camp on Tean. Protection from the prevailing south-westerly winds was provided by the hill behind in Area 1.

which provided good protection from the prevailing south-westerly winds. The wall of a building such as a barn would do equally well. The construction of the tents also needs to be taken into account and, in general, the tougher and more streamlined their design the better. To avoid flooding, a shallow trench should always be dug round the edge of each tent to carry away rain water draining off the top. Concerning sleeping equipment, the main requirement is a warm sleeping bag. It is possible to sleep on the ground using a groundsheet but infinitely preferable to use a light camp bed. It should be remembered that heat loss at night occurs just as much from below as from above, so it is important to have plenty of insulation underneath.

On an expedition of only a few weeks, cooking is unlikely to loom large in the day's affairs. However, with a little ingenuity and an elementary cook book, it is surprising what can be achieved with a primus (paraffin) stove or a ring using bottled gas. A small oven (the shape of a large biscuit tin, with a shelf) can add greatly to the pleasures of meals, for instance by the baking of scones. For comfortable feeding and working, folding chairs will be required. It is a curious fact how many habitual campers fail to appreciate the simple truth that one's camp is one's home (albeit a temporary one) and that the same rules of behaviour, cleanliness, and hygiene apply as in more permanent circumstances. Proper arrangements for latrines and the digging of a suitable rubbish pit (remember rats!) are obvious necessities. But most important of all is the dictum that time spent on public relations is never wasted. It is worth remembering that most farmers and landowners are kindly folk and many are excellent naturalists; the majority will readily give permission to go on their land. Living on an uninhabited island like Tean for a fortnight or so one becomes curiously possessive, to the extent that intruders, even visits by the owner himself, can be resented. No doubt this is just a manifestation of native instincts but in exhibiting them, we must not lose sight of the fact that when tenanting a camp site we are someone else's guests, and only temporary guests at that.

During expeditions of the kind described here it usually happens that scientific work and domesticities do not occupy the whole of the time available. Inclement weather is likely on occasions and there may well be odd hours in the evening that are free for other things. To make the most of such situations there is much to be said for having a second interest which can be pursued on and off as circumstances permit. Professor Ford and I have found that archaeology dovetails well into ecological genetics. The Isles of Scilly supported appreciable Iron Age and Dark Age populations, and we spent many pleasant hours excavating Iron Age hut circles and the supposed sixth-century chapel of St Thiona after whom the island of Tean is named.

3

𝕃𝕃𝕃𝕃𝕃𝕃𝕃𝕃𝕃𝕃𝕃𝕃𝕃𝕃𝕃𝕃𝕃𝕃𝕃𝕃𝕃𝕃𝕃𝕃𝕃𝕃

The mainland stabilizations

Our discovery of the spot-distributions in the meadow brown on Tean provoked a number of questions. What was the situation on the other islands of Scilly? Could it be that we had a parallel here with Darwin's findings among the finches of the Galapagos Islands? These questions and others arising from them will be considered further in Chapter 5. But there was another set of questions to which, at the time, we had no lead whatever, relating to the pattern of spotting on the British mainland. Indeed, did any pattern exist? For convenience, and also to keep the project within bounds, we decided to confine our investigations for the time being to southern England. But even with this degree of restriction, the prospect of collecting meadow browns across the southern counties as well as doing our work in Scilly appeared daunting. We therefore decided to seek the help of collaborators, both individuals and institutions, particularly schools. The outcome was a range of samples varying in size from 50 to over 100, of both males and females from south-west Cornwall, mid-Devon, Somerset, Wiltshire, Oxford, War-wickshire, Kent, and Suffolk. Scoring the samples for spotting produced an extraordinary result. Regarding spot-distribution, the pattern everywhere (excluding the Cornish sample) was the same (Fig. 6). While males were more or less typical of the situation we had already encountered on Tean (unimodal at 2 spots), the females exhibited a pattern entirely new to us—unimodal with the maxi-mum (about 60 per cent) at 0 spots. A second finding of some interest was that within the range of female samples collected for

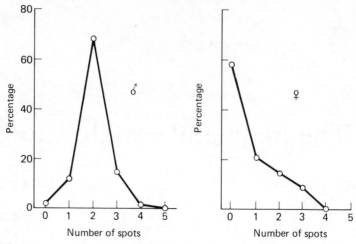

Figure 6   Spot-distribution of the meadow brown in southern England.

us there was a strong resemblance, as is shown by a statistical test ($P < 0.5$).

The Cornish sample came from Feock (near Falmouth) and was peculiar, the spotting being quite distinct from the other seven counties of England (Fig. 7). Thus, while the male frequencies were approximately similar to all the others (unimodal at 2 spots),

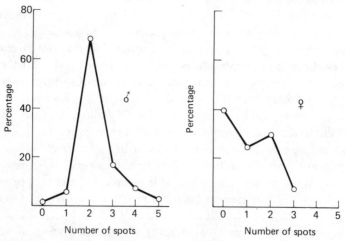

Figure 7   Spotting in meadow browns from south-west Cornwall.

female spotting was bimodal with the larger mode (about 40 per cent) at 2 spots and the smaller (about 30 per cent) at 0. This was almost exactly intermediate between the English form (Fig. 6) and that on Tean (Fig. 5).

Leaving aside for the present the question of any possible relationship between meadow brown populations in south-west Cornwall and the Isles of Scilly (discussed further in Chapter 5), these findings raised a whole new set of important questions. Was the apparent existence of unimodality in the spots of female meadow browns across southern England and bimodality in south-west Cornwall merely the result of inadequate sampling; could the situation be confirmed from more extensive investigations in other populations? If this was, indeed, the established pattern of spot-distribution, in what circumstances did unimodality change into bimodality? Could the existence of a distinctive form of spotting in the west be indicative of a break-up of the stabilization existing elsewhere as the animal approached the limits of its range?

Much of the next two years' work was spent in attempting to clarify the position in the south. With the aid of an increased number of helpers it soon became clear as a result of wider and repeated sampling that the meadow brown populations of southern England did, in fact, represent a stabilization of spot pattern, the males being unimodal at 2 spots and the females at 0 (referred to hereafter as the Southern English, or SE form).[14, 15] The degree of uniformity was all the more remarkable when we remember that the area includes some of the greatest variations in temperature, rainfall, and geology to be found in Britain.

Having established the existence of a Southern English spot-stabilization, it now seemed to us important to turn our attention to the nature of the change-over in female spotting from unimodality to bimodality, as indicated by our earlier sample from Feock, and to discover if this was more than just a localized occurrence. Variable species of animals and plants frequently exhibit gradients of variation (clines) which can be quite short, covering a few hundred metres, or may extend over hundreds of kilometres. Thus, the average colour of the dark arches moth which we studied on Cara (Chapter 1) is predominantly blackish in the north but becomes progressively lighter in more southerly populations. Our hypothesis for female meadow brown spotting was therefore that

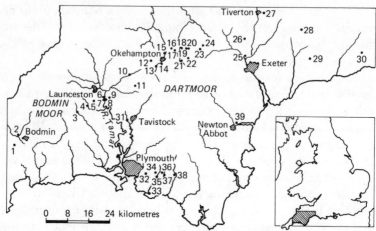

Figure 8   Map of part of south-west England showing some of our sampling areas. 1: Lanivet, 2: Dunmere, 3: Beriowbridge, 4: Larrick Mill, 5: East and West Larrick, 6: Tamar West Flood Plain, 7: Tamar East Flood Plain, 8: Pilistreet, 9: Kelly, 10: Wrixhill Bridge, 11: Lydford, 12: Maddaford, 13: Meldon, 14: Okehampton Golf Course, 15: Abbeyford, 16: Hatherton, 17: Sampford Courtenay, 18: Taw Mill, 19: Thornes Itton, 20: Itton Moor, 21: South Tawton, 22: Powlesland, 23: Hilldown, 24: Walson Barton, 25: Upton Pyne, 26: Raddon, 27: Tiverton, 28: Broadhembury, 29: Gittisham, 30: Hawkchurch, 31: Lumburn, 32: Haye Farm, 33: Noss Mayo, 34: Tuxton, 35: Efford, 36: Lee Mill Bridge, 37: Popples Bridge, 38: Thornham, 39: Newton Abbot.

if any widespread transition from unimodality to bimodality were to occur, it would do so gradually.

Previous evidence had suggested that the meadow brown population at Okehampton (Devon), about 32 km from the Cornish border, was Southern English, and so it proved to be when we visited the area in 1952. Thence we moved westwards another 18 km to Lydford (Fig. 8) which also proved to be Southern English, as was Holsworthy, 32 km to the north. Crossing the river Tamar, we continued our transect westwards to a good locality for meadow browns at Lewannick, some 20 km from Lydford. Scoring our samples, the males proved to be unimodal at 2 spots as usual, but, to our astonishment, the females were now bimodal at 0 and 2 (hereafter called the East Cornish, or EC type). It was now imperative that we should discover in the limited time available whether this East Cornish spot pattern was more widespread.

Table 3 Female spot-distributions of the meadow brown in west Devon and east Cornwall (1952) showing the east–west transition from Southern English (SE) to East Cornish (EC) patterns.

| | | Spots | | | | | | |
	Locality	0	1	2	3	4	5	Total
SE	Okehampton	36	9	5	3	–	–	53
SE	Lydford	21	12	3	–	–	–	36
SE	Holsworthy	10	2	2	–	–	–	14
EC	Lewannick	28	17	21	7	–	–	73
EC	Lanivet	30	16	18	7	1	–	72

Accordingly, we moved another 30 km westwards to Lanivet where the previous findings were repeated. These exciting results were of such significance in shaping the pattern of our later research that they are summarized in Table 3.

It is worth pointing out that the localities at Lewannick and Lanivet were very different, being situated at the east and west extremities of Bodmin Moor which constituted a formidable barrier between them, consisting of wild, windswept highland inimical to colonization by the meadow brown. In spite of this degree of isolation the populations in the two localities proved to have remarkably similar spotting ($P > 0.9$) suggesting that, as in the rest of southern England, variations in spot pattern transcend climatic and other environmental changes. The abrupt change-over from SE to EC spotting between Lydford and Lewannick in a distance of only 21 km threw new and unexpected light on our hypothesis regarding the existence of a cline of variation. If we were, indeed, dealing with a cline, it must be an exceedingly steep one!

Meanwhile, we felt that there was a further pressing problem needing attention. So far our investigations of the meadow brown in the West Country had been confined almost exclusively to the central area north of Dartmoor. But were the phenomena we were observing peculiar to that part of Devon and Cornwall or was the situation repeated further south?

Like Bodmin Moor, Dartmoor is a great granite intrusion creating formidable highlands in central Devon and Cornwall (Fig. 9). The area is windswept and lacking in shelter, and many of the

Table 4　Female spot-distributions of the meadow brown in Devon and Cornwall south of Dartmoor (1952; including two earlier samples) showing the transition from Southern English (SE) to East Cornish (EC) patterns.

| | Locality | Spots | | | | | | |
		0	1	2	3	4	5	Total
SE	Newton Abbot (S Devon)	47	31	10	4	1	–	93
SE	Noss Mayo (SE of Plymouth)	15	8	1	–	–	–	24
SE	Plymstock (1951) (S of Plymouth)	34	14	4	2	–	–	54
EC	Plymouth (North)	47	22	31	4	1	–	105
EC	Roborough (NW of Plymouth)	21	14	18	3	–	–	56
EC	Feock (1950) (Falmouth, Cornwall)	39	24	29	7	–	–	99

species of grasses that grow there are unsuitable as food for the larvae of the meadow brown. As a result, the density of the insect on the moor is very low and there are wide areas where it is absent altogether, so that Dartmoor provides an effective ecological barrier between north and south.

A partial answer to our question regarding the meadow brown populations occupying an east–west transect to the south of Dartmoor was fortunately provided for us by a series of samples which helpers kindly collected. These ranged from Newton Abbot and the Plymouth area to Falmouth (Cornwall) and are summarized in Table 4. As in the central transect, so here there appeared to be an aprupt change-over from Southern English spotting to East Cornish in the vicinity of Plymouth.

A word is needed at this point concerning our findings in the extreme west of Cornwall. As we have seen, the windswept areas of Dartmoor and Bodmin Moor (Fig. 9) effectively prohibit colonization and movement of the meadow brown. The population occupying the Land's End peninsula is thus largely isolated from those inhabiting the rest of Cornwall. It is also cut off from the population of the sandhills in the north by the Hayle estuary. On

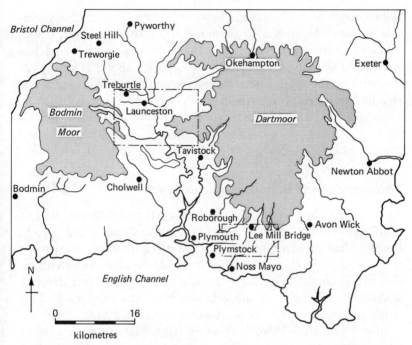

Figure 9 Map of east Cornwall and west Devon; ground over 200 m is shaded. (The rectangular areas around Launceston and south of Dartmoor are elaborated in Figs 10 and 12.)

the Penwith peninsula itself the butterfly proved to be quite common and we found that it occupied an isolated area of about 20 km × 13 km. We were now fast approaching the limits of the animal's range and were therefore justified in our hypothesis that the population might exhibit some unusual features. And so it proved. The distribution of female spotting in these butterflies was

Table 5 Female spot-distributions in west Cornwall (1952).

Localities	Spots						
	0	1	2	3	4	5	Total
Penberth	10	19	25	14	–	–	68
Pendeen	15	20	27	6	2	–	70
Total	25	39	52	20	2	–	138

unlike anything we had seen elsewhere, being approximately similar to the male, with a single mode at 2 spots. However, it was evidently more variable than in the male, the mode being less marked. Two samples collected in localities about 11 km apart, Penberth on the south cost and Pendeen on the north, are summarized in Table 5 and comparison shows them to be similar $(P > 0.3)$.

So here we had evidence of yet a third kind of meadow brown spot-stabilization with the females unimodal at 2. This we called West Cornish (WC).

Discovery of the boundary phenomenon

At this stage (the end of 1952) many fascinating problems faced us both in the Scillies and on the English mainland; but it had already become clear that with our limited resources we would have to be selective. Accordingly, Professor Ford and I decided to concentrate our efforts in the Scillies, for it was there that all our detailed findings relating to the meadow brown had so far been made. This work and the outcomes from it will be described in Chapter 5.

It was not until 1956, four years later, that we were able to resume our studies on the mainland. By now our research team had been augmented by Professor Kennedy McWhirter and Dr Robert Creed. Their arrival was most welcome, not only for the diversity of viewpoints they contributed but also because the extent of the meadow brown research had grown well beyond the capacity of two people.

Outstanding among our problems in the West Country was the nature of the transition from the Southern English stabilization characterized by females unimodal at 0 spots to the East Cornish pattern with females bimodal at 0 and 2. The decision facing us was whether to choose the central transect north of Dartmoor or the southern, since samples previously obtained from both had revealed the same striking and abrupt changes in spotting pattern. We unhesitatingly selected the first alternative for it was in this area that we had collected in the past so we were already well acquainted with its ecology. A particular objection to the southern transect was that the transitional area appeared to be in the vicinity of Plymouth which, with its extensive suburbs, might have presented great problems in obtaining adequate samples of butterflies.

Work undertaken four years earlier had shown that the likely transition area would be between Lydford (SE) and Lewannick (EC), the distance between them being no more than 21 km. Our West Country expedition this year consisted of Professors Ford and McWhirter, although all of us had had a hand in planning the overall strategy. The scheme we had agreed was first to establish the two end-points of the transect; it was hoped that these would be at Lydford in the east and Lewannick to the west. A cross-country route would them be taken from east to west, sampling continuously until a change took place.

Obtaining samples at Lydford[16] (Fig. 8) and Okehampton posed no difficulties and the results showed, as expected, that the SE pattern of spotting was still evident, but with the high mode at 0 somewhat reduced. As we were shortly to discover, this was a 'second order' variation (subsequently called New English) which will be considered separately later. On arriving at the previous site at Lewannick it was found to be ploughed up and destroyed as a habitat for meadow browns—the sort of problem we frequently encounter due to the vicissitudes of agricultural practice. However, a nearby locality at Trekelland (Inny) Bridge over the river Inny (Fig. 10) supported a large population of insects, a sample of 104 females exhibiting typical bimodality in accordance with the EC pattern.

Having established the two ends of the transect, the traverse from east to west could now begin. It was decided to work westwards from Lydford and to divide the distance into three blocks of about 6 km each. The first stop was at Chillaton where the sample proved to be typically unimodal. An advance of a further 6.5 km led to the flood plain of the river Tamar on the west side of the river, just into Cornwall. Here again (at Hexworthy), the female sample proved typically Southern English. Ford and McWhirter were now little more than 10 km from the Inny Bridge where the population was known to be East Cornish; but still no sign of a change. Accordingly, they decided to divide the remaining distance into two approximately equal parts, so far as the terrain allowed. The ground in that area is very irregular and west of the Tamar valley it rises, at first steeply and later more gradually, until within about 450 m of the Inny where it drops down steeply to the river. They continued to move westwards in the direction of Larrick,

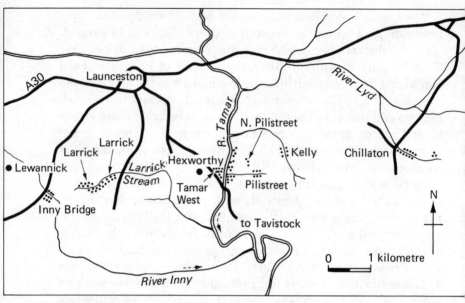

Figure 10   Map of the central transect in which we studied the transition from Southern English to East Cornish spot patterns. The localities where samples were obtained are indicated by dots.

making for the point where the road running south from Launceston crosses the Larrick Stream (Fig. 10). They were now less than 3 km from the population that was known to be East Cornish—and still no change. Whereupon they decided to score their samples of meadow browns, as far as was possible, field by field. A succession of five fields provided a sample of 82 males and 38 females, and they sat down and scored their spotting. It was unquestionably Southern English!

They now climbed through a hedge and proceeded westwards across the next field. It was a large field and the greater part of it was flat, but it sloped steeply down to the stream on its northern side. As they advanced, making a rough assessment of spot-values on the way, they became aware that a change in spot-distribution had at last occurred. They proceeded to collect a further field westwards by which time the sample was 59 males and 41 females. The result was spectacular, confirming the rough assessment made while collecting. The females were completely East Cornish and homogeneous with the sample from Inny Bridge ($P > 0.9$) while being heterogeneous compared with the Larrick insects ($P = 0.05$–0.02). The males, on the other hand, showed no such clear distribution reinforcing the view, already suggested by our earlier data, that for them, spotting is not a clear criterion distinguishing between the EC and SE stabilizations. The results of this extraordinary traverse are summarized in Table 6.

Table 6 Female spot-distributions of the meadow brown in west Devon and east Cornwall (1956) showing the boundary between Southern English (SE) and East Cornish (EC) populations.

| | | *Spots* | | | | | | |
	Locality	0	1	2	3	4	5	Total
SE	Okehampton	45	29	20	5	–	–	99
SE	Lydford	50	27	20	11	–	–	108
SE	Chillaton	38	18	13	6	3	–	78
SE	Tamar West (Hexworthy)	30	19	9	5	1	1	65
SE	East Larrick	20	11	6	1	–	–	38
EC	West Larrick	16	6	13	5	1	–	41
EC	Inny Bridge (Lewannick)	44	18	30	10	2	–	104

Far from the cline which we had postulated, the change-over from one stabilization to another had taken place abruptly in a matter of a few yards, almost at a single hedge! Not that this formed a physical barrier to movement, for the meadow browns were observed to be flying freely from one side to the other. Evidently, the Southern English and East Cornish forms of the butterfly which had remained so stable to the east, and westwards over mainly the whole length of Cornwall, had formed a shallow interface at this point, remaining distinct in spite of the absence of any discernible ecological barrier. We named this the boundary phenomenon.

When examining our results afterwards, as Robert Creed first pointed out, they were even more peculiar than we had realized at the time. In a normal cline of variation we would expect, as we approached a particular point from opposite directions, that the

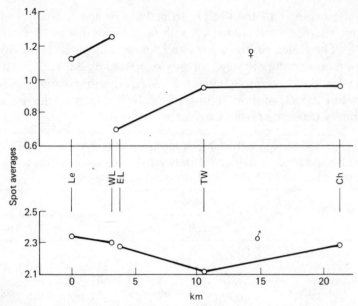

Figure 11   Spot averages in the meadow brown populations at the boundary between East Cornish and Southern English stabilizations in 1956. The females exhibit a reverse cline but the males do not (see text). Le = Lewannick; WL = West Larrick; EL = East Larrick; TW = Tamar West (Hexworthy); Ch = Chillaton.

populations concerned would increasingly resemble one another. But when we compared the spotting of the females along the whole transect from Okehampton to Inny Bridge the difference between the SE and EC types proved to be greatest at the boundary between them. Instead of a cline, we had found a 'reverse cline'. This is best expressed diagrammatically (Fig. 11) by introducing a new parameter of spotting, the spot average. For any sample or comparable set of samples this is obtained by totalling the spots present (scoring one wing only, as usual) and dividing by the number of individuals. Thus Southern English females with about 60 per cent at 0 spots will have a lower spot average than East Cornish females with a lower value at 0 and a higher one at 2 spots. Similarly males, with their high mode at 2 spots, have a higher spot average than females. Reference to Fig. 11 shows the extraordinary discontinuity between the female populations of East and West Larrick, a difference which was not, however, reflected in the males.

How were we to interpret these peculiar and quite unexpected results? One plausible explanation of the difference between east and west was that in the past there had existed some large geographic barrier between them such as an area of forest. This had effectively separated the two sets of populations which had evolved in isolation, becoming adapted to somewhat differing sets of environmental conditions. In so doing they could have developed a degree of genetic discontinuity which had survived long after the physical barrier had been removed. The weakness of this hypothesis was the lack of evidence that any such barrier had ever existed in the area in question. An alternative explanation which avoided this difficulty was that in the course of time the butterfly populations occupying the area of the Penwith peninsula had gradually pushed eastwards while those of the south of England had extended westwards. Both groups would have been adjusted to a very different set of environmental conditions and could therefore have evolved a degree of genetic isolation. The barrier therefore represented the interface between the two due to partial inter-sterility, a phenomenon well known to occur in other animal species. However, subsequent findings were to dispel these ideas and set us thinking on very different lines.

The boundary: subsequent findings

It was obviously imperative that the previous year's work on the central transect should be repeated, if only to confirm the existence of the boundary phenomenon and to establish its permanence. Accordingly, three of us set off at the end of July 1957, our first aim being, as before, to establish the two ends of the transect. The population of meadow browns at Chillaton proved to be typically Southern English, as expected, while that at Inny Bridge was East Cornish. Working from east to west we descended onto the flood plain of the river Tamar and collected near the west bank as before (Fig. 10). To our surprise, female spotting now proved to be bimodal and Cornish. The East Larrick sample was also bimodal so evidently it had not changed since the previous year. It was now a question of retreating eastwards and we found a good locality at Kelly, just under 5 km west of Chillaton. This was Southern English so we advanced westwards a further 1.5 km to Pilistreet where the population of females was still unimodal at 0. We were now approaching the woods which border the Tamar flood plain to the east and obtained a further sample about 150 m north (N Pilistreet) which was still Southern English. Below we could see the west Tamar locality which we knew to be East Cornish, being separated from it by the eastern flood plain, no more than 170 m wide. Here, we manged to accumulate a good sample of females which proved to be intermediate in spotting between Cornish and English. Applying statistical tests, we showed it to be both distinct from the other Southern English samples ($P < 0.02$) and from the East Cornish samples ($P < 0.05$). The results for 1957 are summarized in Table 7.

Table 7   Female spot-distributions of the meadow brown in west Devon and east Cornwall (1957) showing the boundary between Southern English (SE) and East Cornish (EC). The intermediate population (I) is 'flat-topped' at 1 and 2 spots.

		Spots						
	Locality	0	1	2	3	4	5	Total
SE	Chillaton	27	19	10	5	–	–	61
SE	Kelly	50	23	15	10	2	–	100
SE	Pilistreet	51	20	8	6	–	–	85
SE	N Pilistreet	26	11	8	4	1	–	50
I	Tamar East (170 m wide)	67	36	34	5	–	–	142
EC	Tamar West	84	32	41	12	–	–	169
EC	East Larrick	27	3	9	5	1	–	45
EC	Inny Bridge (Lewannick)	80	23	43	8	1	–	155

Subsequent comparisons of spot averages in the female samples showed that the reverse cline which we had detected the previous year was still present but had now shifted about 9 km eastwards to the vicinity of the Pilistreet sample. The work in 1957 had thus added two important new components to our knowledge of the meadow brown. First the interface between spot-stabilizations did not occupy a permanent position but could shift its location from one year to the next. A second finding of somewhat lesser importance was that while the discontinuity between stabilizations could be abrupt (as in 1956), intermediate situations occupying a limited range (as in 1957) might also occur from time to time. These characteristics have proved a feature of our findings ever since (up to 1981).

The fact that the boundary was movable and not established as a permanency at a particular point, effectively disposed of our previous hypothesis based on the idea of some degree of genetic discontinuity between two evolving stabilizations. Clearly, any fluctuation such as we found to have taken place in so short a time could not be accounted for in this manner. As we shall see in Chapter 5, we had by now accumulated a great deal of evidence from widespread studies in the Isles of Scilly strongly supporting the idea that spotting in the meadow brown must be closely related to the insect's survival and probably acts as an indicator of other characteristics associated with different values and combinations of spotting. We did not know the precise nature of its adaptive significance, but it was clear that whatever it was, it must be under the influence of powerful selective forces enabling optimum values to be achieved in a variety of different ecological situations. Translating these ideas into a mainland context, it seemed to us that, throughout southern England, the diversity of existing ecological conditions must have brought about the evolution of an optimum form in both sexes manifest in the Southern English stabilization. But in the west, as the butterfly neared the limit of its range, the main stabilization had broken down, giving way to a number of sub-stabilizations such as East Cornish and West Cornish in response to the increased diversity of environments, such as those of the Penwith peninsula, to which the species was less well adjusted. Important additional evidence of the action of selective forces in controlling spotting was provided by the reverse cline effect which had been a feature of the boundary area in 1956 and 1957. Indeed, it was hard to imagine how its occurrence could have been explained in any other way. A selectionist approach to our work on the meadow brown thus coloured our thinking increasingly in subsequent years.

Our work on this butterfly illustrates admirably the strengths and limitations of the kind of ecological fieldwork we undertook, indeed, of fieldwork in general. Thus it soon became clear that observations of the animal in the wild were unlikely to contribute significantly to the solution of problems concerning the nature of the adaptive advantages and disadvantages associated with different kinds of spotting. On the other hand we also needed information of a more long-term kind regarding the magnitude of the problems we were tackling; were we dealing with stable or fluctuating situations; if fluctuating, what was the magnitude of the fluctuations; were there any discernible ecological conditions tending to promote stability or instability of spot-stabilizations? The adequate monitoring of a diverse situation such as that of the

Plate 14   Scoring meadow browns. Left to right: Professor Dowdeswell, Professor McWhirter, Dr Creed, and Professor Ford. Dr Creed is recording the results; the rest are determining the spot-values and calling them out in turn.

meadow brown populations in Britain is a never-ending process but nonetheless a rewarding one. This explains why the observations begun in 1950 are still in progress some thirty years later. Our studies of the meadow brown must rank as some of the most continuous and extensive ever carried out on a single animal species. Our expeditions have varied in size from year to year—a typical roadside scene is recorded in Plate 14 where scoring is in progress. The usual division of labour adopted has been for one person to record and the remainder to determine the spot-values and call them out. In the event of a doubtful specimen due to abnormal spotting or some sort of damage, a consensus view was obtained. Our work has been greatly aided by many helpers, some of whom have joined us for only short periods, while others, in particular Mr and Mrs S Beaufoy, have regularly provided invaluable assistance. We have also been honoured by visits from a number of distinguished biologists from overseas such as Professor T. Dobzhansky and Professor Ernst Mayer from the United States. We were able to demonstrate to them the occurrence of the boundary phenomenon and the features associated with it, including the sudden change of one type of stabilization to another.

It would be inappropriate here to attempt a survey of the findings of each of the many visits that some or all of us have made to the West Country since the discovery of the boundary phenomenon. However, certain generalizations have been established, of such importance that they need to be summarized.

1. The overwhelming picture emerging from our studies of meadow brown spotting in southern England is one of extraordinary stability. True, there have been temporary fluctuations in the two great stabilizations of a 'second order' kind (to be discussed shortly), usually correlated with extreme climatic change such as drought. But these have taken place within the broad framework of the main stabilizations and the spot-values have invariably returned to their established patterns.

2. As we have seen, the position of the boundary between the East Cornish and Southern English stabilizations turned out to be a dynamic affair and not a fixed entity as we had originally supposed. Indeed, its annual mobility proved to be far greater than we ever imagined, extending on occasions a maximum distance eastwards of some 70 km into west Dorset and retreating westwards again a year or so later. This effectively disposed of any possible explanation based on the existence of some sort of genetic discontinuity between the two stabilizations.

3. The nature of the boundary has also varied somewhat from year to year within certain limits. On occasions it has been abrupt, occupying a few metres only, as we first found it at Larrick in 1956. A typical example in later years has been Itton Moor (see Fig. 8) about 11 km north-east of Okehampton which supports a large population of meadow browns. In 1964, 1965, and again

in 1979 we established the boundary within a few metres (Plate 15) where no physical barrier existed, this separating the population into Itton West (EC) and Itton East (SE).

On other occasions the nature of the boundary has proved more diffuse, involving intermediate forms of female spotting of a flat-topped kind with more or less equal values at 1 and 2 spots. Sometimes the transitional area has occupied only a few hundred metres but on occasions it has extended further, covering several kilometres.

Plate 15   The barrier at Itton Moor, near Okehampton, Devon, in 1979. The boundary between the East Cornish (left) and the Southern English (right) stabilizations ran approximately along a line from the gate in the foreground to the row of trees in the middle distance.

4. In periods of rapid ecological adjustment to changing environmental conditions, for instance as a result of a drought, it is hardly surprising to find that not all butterfly colonies adjust at the same speed. Thus, among populations in the process of changing from say unimodality to bimodality, it is not uncommon to find pockets that respond at a different rate from the

rest. Some of these are now well known to us, having exhibited this tendency on a number of occasions. We would naturally look for the most extreme examples in places subject to a good deal of ecological isolation which are, in effect, islands on land. Such a locality is Rowden Moor (see Fig. 8) about 6 km north-east of Okehampton, a small area of grassland of about 2 hectares bounded by trees, supporting a small population of butterflies which must be largely isolated. The terrain is peculiar in that at least half of it is boggy with a range of coarse grasses unsuitable as food for the meadow brown. On a number of occasions this small colony has been out of step, so to speak, with others in the surrounding area. Thus in 1972, a year of general instability, female spotting at Rowden Moor was clearly unimodal while that of populations only a few kilometres away on either side was either flat-topped or bimodal.

5. While populations in the south-west have undergone periods of instability and temporary change, others further east have remained completely stable. An outstanding example is that at Ipswich which Mr S. Beaufoy has kindly sampled annually on our behalf for a period of almost 30 years. Throughout this long time female spotting has invariably remained Southern English, thus providing a splendid backstop for the rest of our work. In the other direction, the populations towards Land's End have also been fairly regularly visited but not to the same extent as Ipswich. Here again, a stable West Cornish pattern has prevailed.

The southern transect

Samples of meadow browns collected for us in 1952 and earlier from the transect to the south of Dartmoor and Bodmin Moor, had suggested an abrupt transition in female spotting similar to that in the north. This had occurred in the vicinity of Plymouth. Ideally, the detailed study of the two transects should have proceeded simultaneously but this would have been an undertaking beyond our resources. The central transect was therefore accorded preference, largely because we were already familiar with much of its ecology. Now that we had discovered so much about the boundary phenomenon in the north it was time to reopen the question whether a similar situation obtained in the south. Or was the position in the central transect peculiar to that part of southern England only?

A limited range of samples obtained in 1958 had suggested that the area of transition from SE spotting to EC had moved substantially eastwards from the area of Plymouth to somewhere between Lee Mill Bridge and Newton Abbot (see Fig. 9). This information provided the starting point for our work in 1959. The first step was

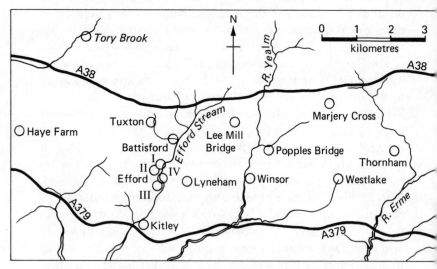

Figure 12   Localities where samples were obtained along the southern transect (1959–60).

to establish our two backstops. The female samples from Noss Mayo and Lee Mill Bridge (Fig. 9) proved to be identical ($P > 0.8$) and typically bimodal (EC).[17] Mr and Mrs Beaufoy had collected a large sample from Newton Abbot which was SE. Avon Wick (Fig. 9), some 15 km east of Lee Mill Bridge, was also clearly unimodal (SE). Tantalizingly, the next three samples at Bittaford, Harford, and Ludbrook proved to be somewhat indeterminate with tendencies towards a flat-topped distribution at 1 and 2 spots, rather reminiscent of the situation at Tamar West (Hexworthy) in the north in 1957. However, the large sample at Thornham (Fig. 12) indicated clearly the extension of the SE stabilization thus far.

We were now within 3.5 km of the EC population at Lee Mill Bridge and suitable collecting sites were becoming hard to find. After a considerable effort which included dragging a rope across one field after another in order to stir up such few butterflies as there were, we obtained a sample at Popples Bridge which was clearly EC. When the females are compared with Lee Mill Bridge and Noss Mayo, they are obviously similar ($P > 0.8$). The results of the year's work are summarized in Table 8.

Table 8 Female spot-distributions in the meadow brown from the southern transect (1959). The localities are arranged in order from east to west and show the transition from Southern English (SE) to East Cornish (EC).

	Locality	Spots						
		0	1	2	3	4	5	Total
SE	Newton Abbot	44	16	10	10	1	–	81
SE	Avon Wick	47	14	12	7	3	1	84
?	Bittaford	33	11	14	8	1	–	67
SE?	Harford	18	7	6	2	–	–	33
SE?	Ludbrook	9	5	3	4	1	–	22
SE	Thornham	50	21	17	10	4	–	102
SE	Marjery Cross	13	7	5	6	–	–	31
EC	Popples Bridge	21	8	17	8	1	–	55
EC	Lee Mill Bridge	28	12	23	5	–	–	68
EC	Noss Mayo	38	15	28	7	3	–	91

We searched anxiously for another locality between Thornham and Popples Bridge and eventually found a small population at Marjery Cross (Table 8; Fig. 12). The result was inconclusive but with a stong inclination towards SE. We were thus unable to demonstrate the abrupt change-over which had characterized the central transect, not because the spot patterns merged into one another but because the butterfly was more localized in its distribution in a critical part of the transect. The reason for this patchiness can be explained by reference to the map (Fig. 9) from which it will be seen that the rivers and their tributaries run predominantly from north to south, the high land in between being often unsuitable for colonization by the meadow brown.

The previous year's results provided a strong indication of the kind of discontinuity between the two great spot-stabilizations in the south that we had previously identified further north. It must be remembered that at that time we lacked experience of the range of variations in the boundary phenomenon that we were to encounter later, so the hypothesis we were aiming to test was essentially that of an abrupt change-over such as we had first found at Larrick in the north (Table 6). Accordingly, in the summer of 1960 we decided to commit all our resources to the elucidation of this problem. In contrast with the previous year, Noss Mayo and Lee Mill Bridge which had formerly been EC were now SE, whereas Haye Farm to the west was EC and unchanged. Evidently the boundary lay somewhere between Lee Mill Bridge and Haye Farm (Fig. 12), which are about 6 km apart. Between them is a valley through which runs the Efford Stream (Fig. 12) passing through the hamlet of Efford. At this point the sides of the valley are steep grassy slopes with a hanging wood to the west extending down-

Plate 16   The boundary area of the southern transect at Efford (1960). Efford I (EC) is in the distance identified by the white house. Efford III (SE) is the sloping hill on the left. Efford IV (boundary) is the large field in the middle, bounded by a stream on the left and a road on the right. The distance between Efford I and Efford III is less than 400 m.

wards almost to the stream (Plate 16). In the first field (later named Efford I) the female spot-distribution was strongly bimodal. Efford II to the east of the road yielded only twelve butterflies. Efford III, less than 0.5 km down the valley, supported a large population (see Plate 16; left foreground) the females being clearly SE. The two localities were thus separated by one long field, Efford IV (Plate 16; middle) which, alas, only yielded twenty insects in spite of intensive collecting. These southern results in the vicinity of the boundary are summarized in Table 9.

Once again the boundary area had been located, this time to within a distance of less than 400 m, the dividing line between the two great spot-stabilizations being no more than an open field.

Table 9 Female spot-distributions of the meadow brown in the vicinity of the boundary in the southern transect between Southern English (SE) and East Cornish (EC) stabilizations.

		Spots						
	Locality	0	1	2	3	4	5	Total
SE	Lee Mill Bridge	63	34	17	7	2	1	124
SE	Noss Mayo	75	32	24	10	–	2	143
SE	Battisford	73	50	35	16	–	1	175
SE	Efford III	57	25	17	7	1	–	107
?	Efford IV	8	9	2	–	1	–	20
?	Efford II	6	3	1	2	–	–	12
EC	Efford I	18	11	16	4	–	–	49
EC	Tuxton	33	10	19	9	–	–	71
EC	Haye Farm	46	24	32	2	2	–	106

The meadow brown in Scotland

For administrative and other reasons, the whole of our early work on evolutionary divergence in the meadow brown was confined to the south and south-west of England. Apart from a few samples from Ireland which will be considered further in Chapter 5, we had no idea of the distribution of spotting elsewhere in either sex. We had found abrupt discontinuities in the south between the three stabilizations in transects running east and west: could there be similar differences in a north–south direction? A contribution by

Dr Bruce Foreman and some of his students from the University of Aberdeen was thus of great importance.[18] In order to ensure consistency of scoring procedure so that the results were comparable with those obtained in the south, the butterflies were sent to Oxford and scored by Professor Ford and Professor McWhirter. The results are summarized in Table 10.

Table 10　Samples of meadow browns from north Sutherland (1956) compared with those from three similar localities in southern England (Middleton East, Hampshire; Woolbury Ring, Hampshire; Newton Abbot, Devon). A χ^2 test shows the English samples to be homogeneous: for the males $P > 0.3$ and for the females $P > 0.1$.

		Spots						
Locality	Sex	0	1	2	3	4	5	Total
Sutherland	Male	8	27	101	19	6	–	161
	Female	73	26	6	2	–	–	107
Southern England	Male	6	22	133	44	9	–	214
	Female	191	84	35	5	2	–	317

The spot-distributions of the two groups were clearly similar, with the males unimodal at 2 spots and the females with a high mode at 0. The similarity is confined by a statistical comparison: for the males $P > 0.3$, and for the females $P > 0.1$.

These important results obtained from the north-west extremity of Britain, although somewhat restricted in their coverage, suggested that the Southern English stabilization also extended northwards.

Just as the Scilly Isles represent the westerly limit of the range of the meadow brown, so Scotland marks its northerly distribution. Could it be that the kind of instability we identified in the southwest was repeated in the north as well? The recent work of Dr Paul Brakefield at Liverpool University[19] has been of great importance in helping to resolve this question and has served to complement the earlier limited findings of Dr Foreman and his students.[18] The sampling of numerous populations at both high and low altitudes has revealed the interesting fact that while there is indeed some continuity in spot-distribution between north and south, judged by spot average, there exists a clear-cut cline (gradient of variation) in spot-values. This is illustrated in Table 11.

In the Grampian mountains the species proved to be absent above an altitude of about 300 m. Samples from populations at 165–185 m (Grampians) exhibited high spot averages in both sexes, with bimodality in the females. In contrast, populations in the Sidlaw Hills (185 and 245 m) were characterized by lower spot averages, the females being unimodal and typical of southern England. Evidently, populations in this area showed a readiness to

Table 11 Spot averages of meadow brown populations in southern England and Scotland (after Brakefield).

Area	Number of populations	Mean spot average (male)	Mean spot average (female)
South England	15	2.23	0.82
Central Eastern Scotland	15	2.00	0.74
Central Eastern Scotland (excluding Grampian Mts)	12	1.94	0.63
North Scotland	5	1.89	0.38

adjust to the varying ecological conditions. As was to be expected, spotting in the male remained typically unimodal at 2 but in the Lundie Craggs population (245 m) there was a marked lowering of the spot average due to a greatly increased proportion of one-spot individuals, suggesting that in this high-altitude population environmental conditions were sufficiently extreme to affect adjustment in both sexes.

Of particular interest was a series of samples taken by Brakefield along a transect of 5 km near St Andrews. Whereas the males showed homogeneity throughout the five years of study, the females divided clearly into typical eastern and western forms (Fig. 13). A comparison of the two groups over the five years showed a clearly significant difference between them ($P < 0.001$). While in the first year (1973) there was a sharp boundary separating the two sets of populations, the discontinuity between them, while persisting in

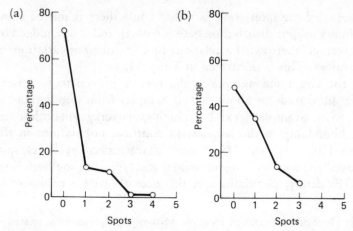

Figure 13   Spot-distributions of female meadow browns on either side of a 5 km transect near St Andrews (Scotland); (a) typical eastern form, (b) typical western form.

the same area, became less sharp throughout the period of study. The St Andrews populations of butterflies thus provided an interesting comparison with those of the south-west and Scillies, suggesting that discontinuities may well be a characteristic feature of the adaptation of meadow brown populations when they near the extremity of their range.

Second order variation

As has been emphasized already, the general picture emerging of variation in the meadow brown was one of stability. Thus the Southern English stabilization extending across the south to the vicinity of the Devon–Cornwall border and northwards into Scotland could be regarded as first order variation, as were the East and West Cornish stabilizations. Yet it was clear that spotting, whatever its significance for the meadow brown, was a character which responded sensitively to ecological change. How else could one explain the observed variations in the position of the boundary and the variety of stabilizations existing in the Isles of Scilly (see Chapter 5)? We might have expected, therefore, that major climatic variations could exert appreciable second order effects within the established framework of first order stability. We were soon to discover that such variation could, in fact, occur and that it might assume two rather different forms.[17]

(a) INTER-SEASONAL VARIATION

In 1956 a wave of high spotting swept through the Southern English stabilization affecting many populations (but by no means all). For convenience we named the resulting second order variations in the females as follows:

(i) *Old English* (OE): the familiar pattern with specimens at 0 spots comprising 60 per cent or more of the total of specimens at 0, 1, and 2 spots; those at 2 spots do not exceed the number at 1 spot.

(ii) *New English* (NE): specimens at 0 spots less than 60 per cent of the total at 0, 1, and 2 spots; specimens at 2 spots do not exceed those at 1 spot.

(iii) *Pseudo-Cornish* (PC): a major mode at 0 spots and a minor mode at 2 spots.

Until 1955, the populations of southern England and east Cornwall had been of the Old English type. But in 1956 many changed to New English and a few even showed a small secondary mode becoming Pseudo-Cornish. Such changes may well have been the result of climatic conditions which had led to an extreme abundance of the butterfly. In 1957, following an abnormally mild winter and a prolonged drought in the spring, the numbers declined and high spotting receded. By 1958 the Southern English population had mostly returned to Old English except in Devon, Somerset, and Dorset, where they tended to remain New English. During this period of change the males also showed some degree of variation. Thus, those with spot numbers in excess of 2 were generally much more common than those with spot numbers less than 2, and some correlation with the three grades of female spot-frequency could be detected.

(b) INTRA-SEASONAL VARIATION

Another quite unexpected aspect of variation in the meadow brown was brought to our attention by Dr J. D. F. Frazer of the Nature Conservancy who also became interested in our work in the late

1950s. While studying colonies of the butterfly on Burham Down in Kent, he discovered that a distinct and statistically significant change took place in both males and females from high spot averages (see p. 123) at the beginning of the emergence to lower values at the middle and end. Subsequent experience showed that intraseasonal shift, as it came to be called, always assumed the same form but was a feature of some colonies and not of others.[17] Thus while it was a regular feature of a population near Winchester it was absent from the colony at Middleton East near Andover, only 16 km away. My studies of the meadow brown in the area of Winchester over a period of eight years amply confirmed the findings elsewhere in the south of England of extreme spot-stability, in so far as first order variation was concerned. The consolidated results are summarized in Table 12.

Table 12   Summary of samples of meadow browns from the Winchester area (1961–8) showing second order variations.

Date	Sex	Spots						Total	Probability	Spot average	Range of variation
		0	1	2	3	4	5				
June–July	Male	16	70	808	260	75	5	1234	$P < 0.01$	2.26	2.12–2.41
August	Male	6	27	413	85	14	2	547	$P > 0.2$	2.15	2.01–2.25
June–July	Female	492	329	209	94	10	–	1134	$P < 0.05$	0.94	0.74–1.21
August	Female	505	198	104	22	2	–	831	$P < 0.001$	0.58	0.42–0.97

The column in Table 12 headed 'Probability' provides information on the similarity of each set of samples, low values of P indicating a high level of intra-seasonal variation. In order to show how this fluctuated over a period of eight seasons, the results are also expressed graphically in Fig. 14. It can be seen that interseasonal fluctuations in the two sexes followed much the same pattern but were greater in the females than in the males. This accorded well with our findings of first order spot-variations elsewhere, the female always proving the more variable sex. Intraseasonal variation followed the same pattern in both sexes, the spot average (Table 12) being high early in the season and low later on. Thus, spotted females comprised 57 per cent of the early samples but only 39 per cent of the late ones. The picture thus

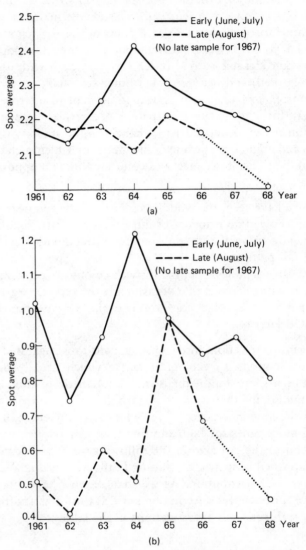

Figure 14 Inter- and intra-seasonal variation in meadow brown populations near Winchester (Hampshire), 1961–8; (a) males, (b) females.

emerging from this long study of an isolated population of meadow browns was one of extreme spot-stability in so far as first order variation was concerned. For eight seasons the males maintained the characteristic high mode at 2 spots while the females were unimodal at 0. However, throughout this time the population showed considerable second order variation both within seasons (intra-seasonal) and between them (inter-seasonal).

The problem facing us now was to attempt to interpret intra-seasonal shift and its curiously patchy occurrence. It appeared to be in some way associated with changes in the stability of populations and might even be one of the means by which such changes came about. This latter idea was confirmed by two opposing sets of data:

(i) As we have seen, the Middleton East population near Winchester showed no evidence of intra-seasonal shift. Significantly, when the wave of high spotting occurred it did not depart from the OE pattern.

(ii) Extensive samples from the Ipswich colony collected for us by Mr Beaufoy showed that occasionally the early emergence was rather highly spotted, conforming to the NE type, but changed to OE later on.

In terms of selection, intra-seasonal shift thus suggested that in some populations an ecological factor which usually operated against high-spotted individuals was simultaneously lifted in some places but not in others so as to disturb the balance only in the first part of the long emergence. This would have the effect of perpetuating more genes for high spotting than usual which would be passed on to the population the following year. This could well have happened at Ipswich, resulting in the observed change from an OE to NE distribution. As we shall see in Chapter 6, strong evidence for powerful selection pressure against high spotting was to be a feature of our investigations in the laboratory.

Spot-placing as an index of variation

So far the parameters used for quantifying and comparing variation in the meadow brown had been spot number and spot average. An attempt was also made to use spot size as an index of change, but in spite of the accumulation of a considerable amount of data, this proved difficult to analyse and the results we obtained appeared to be inconclusive.

However, we had long realised that there might be advantages in scoring spotting in terms of position as well as number. It will be remembered that spots can only occur at certain sites on the hind-wing. In the adult meadow brown of both sexes the outer third of the underside of the hind-wings is lighter in colour than the area nearest the body. This border is divided by the veins of the wings between each of which is a distinct fold (Fig. 1, p. 7). The spots always occur in these folds, with never more than one to each. Although this gives a maximum of seven possible positions, only five of them are commonly occupied (see Fig. 1), thus giving a normal spot-range of 0–5. In addition, the spots are only found in certain combinations and of the ten possible ways in which two spots might occur only three are usually encountered. The most

		◄—— Costal			Anal ——►	
		1	2	3	4	5
	0	–	–	–	–	–
Costal	1	–	●	–	–	–
Anal	1	–	–	–	●	–
Costal	2	●	●	–	–	–
Splay	2	–	●	–	●	–
Anal	2	–	–	–	●	●
Costal	3	●	●	–	●	–
Median	3	–	●	●	●	–
Anal	3	–	●	–	●	●
Costal	4	●	●	●	●	–
Splay	4	●	●	–	●	●
Anal	4	–	●	●	●	●
	5	●	●	●	●	●

Figure 15 Spot-placing most commonly found together with the nomenclature adopted.

frequent arrangements are shown diagrammatically in Fig. 15. The basis of the classification is whether there is a preponderance of spots towards the costal (front) or anal (rear) border of the wing. An equal division represents the 'splay' or 'median' condition. For convenience, bias, or the lack of it, is reflected in the names adopted. Scoring on this basis, which we adopted as long ago as 1958, can be greatly simplified by the use of a pro-forma. The one we have used and which has proved extremely successful is shown in Fig. 16. It will be noted that the sequence of letters on the left-hand side differs slightly in the two sexes. Thus B (Upper Costal 1) with the spot on the first wing fold, occurs only in females, as does K (Cos Med 3) with spots on folds 2 and 3, and the one between. Similarly P (Anal 4) with spots in positions 3, 4, and 5, and on the fold between 2 and 3, is known only in males. The totals for each category are summarized in column GT (Grand Total), while the section for remarks is used for recording other variants such as spotting abnormalities, asymmetries, degree of wear, and so forth.

There are many ways in which an analysis of spot-placing could be undertaken. The publication of a book of essays in honour of Professor Ford's seventieth birthday[20] provided Professor Mc-Whirter and Dr Creed with a timely opportunity for exploring this field further and analysing the considerable volume of data that had by now accumulated.[21] The relative proportions of spot-placing types in different populations revealed several trends. It soon became clear that such trends were common to all spot-number groupings, the degree of presence or absence of say the costal spots being a feature of a whole population applying to both males and females, though in differing degree. McWhirter and Creed therefore decided to quantify spot-placing by means of a 'costality index'. This can be calculated for any population as the proportion, expressed as a percentage, of the total number of costal spots (positions 1 and 2) among those occurring both costally and anally (positions 1, 2, 4, and 5). Thus the spot that is nearly central (position 3) is not included. Referring to Fig. 15, it will be seen that a score of 'Median 3' will comprise one costal and one anal spot (the median spot being omitted). Similarly, 'Anal 4' will include one costal and two anals. It should be noted that the few individuals likely to be encountered having five spots are omitted from this calculation.

MANIOLA JURTINA

Locality: Grid Ref: Date: County:

MALES			Scoring		G T	Remarks
A		0				
C	Cos	1				
D	An	1				
	Other	1				
E	Cos	2				
F	Spl	2C				
G	Spl	2=				
H	Spl	2A				
I	An	2				
	Other	2				
J	Cos	3				
L	Med	3				
M	An	3				
	Other	3				
N	Cos	4				
O	Spl	4				Cos / An
P	An	4				
	Other	4				
Q	Normal	5				
	Other	5				
				Total:		

FEMALES			Scoring		G T	Remarks
A		0				
B	U Cos	1				
C	Cos	1				
D	An	1				
	Other	1				
E	Cos	2				
F	Spl	2C				
G	Spl	2=				
H	Spl	2A				
I	An	2				
	Other	2				
J	Cos	3				
K	Cos Med	3				
L	Med	3				
M	An	3				
	Other	3				
N	Cos	4				
O	Spl	4				Cos / An
	Other	4				
Q	Normal	5				
	Other	5				
				Total:		

Figure 16 Pro-forma used for scoring spot numbers and spot-placing.

Of particular interest in the present context were the findings for the transition zones in the central transect between the three great spot-stabilizations in southern England. A selection of the relevant results is summarized in Table 13.

In the males there is a progressive increase in costality passing westwards from the Southern English stabilization with no apparent discontinuity at the boundary area. The situation in the females is, however, quite different for in the zone where we now know that spot numbers undergo profound change, an appreciable alteration in the costality index also occurred. Thus, whereas the males exhibit a cline of increasing costality passing from east to

Table 13   The costality index for spot-placing in male and female meadow browns within the three spot-stabilizations of southern England (S. England, the Boundary Region and W. Cornwall). For each value the estimate of error is the standard error.

	Costality index	
Locality	Males	Females
Southern England	47.6 ± 0.9	74.5 ± 1.0
Boundary Region, East	48.9 ± 0.5	69.2 ± 0.6
Boundary Region, Central	48.9 ± 0.8	67.0 ± 0.8
Boundary Region, West	49.0 ± 0.5	66.2 ± 0.5
West Cornwall	49.4 ± 1.6	71.2 ± 1.3

west, the females not only show an interruption but a reversal in the boundary region, which is partly retrieved in West Cornwall.

When interpreting these results, it could be argued that if the parameters of spot number and costality index are mutually dependent, then these findings are precisely what we might have expected. As Professor Ford has pointed out,[22] if the two could be shown to be largely independent, the boundary phenomenon would not only be confirmed but its importance would be greatly enhanced in view of its effect on another aspect of spotting. To test this hypothesis we needed a population of butterflies away from the south of England. Such a sample was obtained from Wester Ross where the female spot number (as in Sutherland further north, Table 10), was typically SE being unimodal at 0, and the spot averages in the two sexes were also similar. Yet in spite of these similarities the difference in costality index was extreme: 48.7 for the Scottish females and 74.5 for the English. There is now much additional evidence in support of the view that spot number (or spot average) and costality index are, in a way, different aspects of the same or a similar system of variation. They certainly interact but are not just different measures of the same variant. The fact that in the critical boundary area the females show a marked response in both respects provides powerful confirmation that ecological conditions of a special kind must exist there.

4

The meadow brown in Europe

Our studies of variation in the meadow brown in Britain had established that spot-distribution achieves a remarkable stability even in the face of fluctuating and diverse environments. This was true in both males and females, but since the female was the more variable sex, it provided the better indicator of adjustment to changing situations. We now became aware that while our researches had centred on butterfly populations in southern England and the Scillies, and to a lesser extent in the rest of England, Scotland, and Ireland, we knew next to nothing about the insect's variation throughout the greater part of its range, which extends some 5000 km eastwards from Britain.

A number of questions occurred to us which, if answered, could throw much valuable light on the evolution and status of the butterfly throughout its distribution.

1. How far does the Southern English stabilization extend eastwards?
2. What other stabilizations occur throughout the insect's range in Europe, Asia, and Africa?
3. For how long have these stabilizations existed?
4. In what circumstances (outside Britain) does one form of stabilization change into another?

Arranging for samples of butterflies to be collected throughout this vast area was obviously out of the question. So Professor Kennedy McWhirter and I had recourse to the national collection

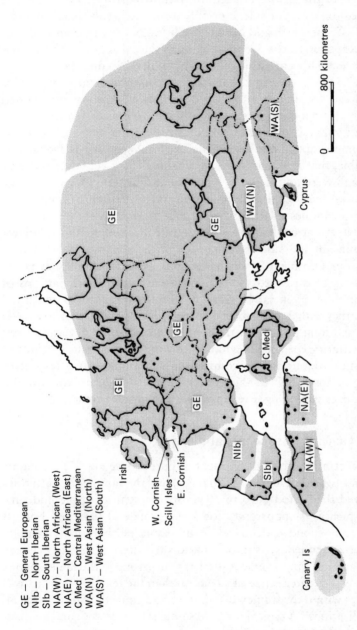

GE – General European
NIb – North Iberian
SIb – South Iberian
NA(W) – North African (West)
NA(E) – North African (East)
C Med – Central Mediterranean
WA(N) – West Asian (North)
WA(S) – West Asian (South)

Figure 17 Spot-stabilizations in the meadow brown throughout its range. The dots indicate the sites of samples.

housed in the British Museum (Natural History). Here, fortune proved to be on our side. Not only were we given valuable help by Mr T. G. Howarth and Mr M. P. Clifton of the Museum staff, but we were soon to discover that many of the collections of butterflies had been made early this century by Walter, Second Baron Rothschild. He held the view that species should be defined on a wide basis and not on just a few 'type' specimens. Accordingly, he had accumulated a considerable series of meadow brown samples from a wide range of localities, summarized on the map in Fig. 17. It was important at the outset for us to make sure, as far as was possible, that the collections represented effectively random samples and were not biased in a particular direction. Our knowledge of the Southern English stabilization and the existence of numerous English samples in the museum collection soon showed that no evident attention had been paid by collectors to the relatively insignificant spots on the underside of the hind-wings. As will be seen, our treatment of the collections as valid samples so far as spots were concerned yielded consistent and distinct patterns of distribution. Even rather small collections were scored and listed since they either contributed to the general picture over a wide area and long periods of time, or suggested some deviation from the pattern expected. Inevitably, this meant a certain sacrifice of statistical rigour in the comparison of samples with respect to their homogeneity. In this context, spot average proved a useful parameter providing a reliable index of general trends.

The General European stabilization

The central part of the continent of Europe (see Fig. 17) is roughly a square of side 2500 km (1500 miles) and the samples of butterflies covered the period 1890 to 1936. Such a span of space and time gave plenty of opportunity for a wide range of variation both at first and second order level. True, some of the female samples showed a tendency, as in Britain, to vary inter-seasonally between high and low spot averages. Perhaps surprisingly, the males tended to show a greater range of variation than the females, but this was always within the framework that we had come to regard as the SE stabilization.[23] A typical range of samples from France and Switzerland is summarized in Table 14.

Table 14 Samples of meadow browns from France and Switzerland (1891-1929).

Locality	Spots						Total	Spot average
	0	1	2	3	4	5		
Male								
Switzerland 1907	–	–	15	6	–	–	21	2.3
France 1929	–	1	13	10	4	1	29	2.7
Digne, France 1908	–	2	7	7	4	–	20	2.7
Royan, France 1924-9	–	1	12	2	1	–	16	2.1
France 1921	–	1	5	3	1	–	10	2.4
Rennes, France 1896; 1905-6	–	–	23	12	5	–	40	2.5
Total of males	–	5	75	40	15	1	136	2.5
Female								
Chateau d'Oex, Switzerland	6	–	1	–	–	–	7	(0.3)
St Martin-Vestubie France	6	2	4	–	–	–	12	0.9
Vernet les Bains, France 1891-6	86	21	21	4	2	1	135	0.7
Vernet les Bains, France 1909	13	5	7	2	–	1	28	1.1
Digne, France 1908	11	2	1	1	–	–	15	0.5
Royan, France 1924-9	9	3	4	2	–	–	18	1.0
St Jean de Monts, France 1921	35	11	4	2	–	–	52	0.5
Rennes, France 1896; 1905-6	28	8	7	2	–	–	45	0.6
Total of females	194	52	49	13	2	2	312	0.7

The picture emerging of spot distribution in Europe placed the Southern English stabilization in a new perspective. No longer could it be regarded as an entity on its own but rather as the western extremity of the General European (GE) stabilization extending some 2500 km eastwards almost to the extremity of the insect's range.

Peripheral stabilizations

At the periphery of the range of the meadow brown on the edge of the GE stabilization the familiar spot-distributions started to break down, sometimes quite abruptly, forming a whole new range of patterns often differing markedly from one another. Thus samples from the northern area of the Iberian peninsula showed a marked divergence from GE, as did those from Portugal north of the Monchique and from Andalusia further south. Samples from the Central Mediterranean showed trends in the same direction as the Iberian peninsula but evidence was insufficient to detect any form of stabilization. As we shall see, as far as Italy is concerned, this deficiency was later to be remedied by the work of Dr Valerio Scali and his associates at the University of Pisa. The Canary Islands showed affinity with the North Iberian patterns but differed markedly from those of the nearby African coast. Here the division could be made between the west including Morocco, Tangier, and the Atlas mountains, and the area of Algeria and Tunisia in the east. Restricted samples from the extreme easterly limits of the animal's range suggested that here again a distinction was needed between West Asia North typified by Turkey, and West Asia South including Syria and Kurdistan. Clearly, much interesting work still needs to be done in these peripheral zones; some of their typical spot-distributions are shown graphically in Fig. 18.

The geography of variation

The overall picture of variation in the meadow brown throughout its range that emerges from a study of samples throughout Europe, West Asia, and North Africa covering a span of roughly 60 years, is of a series of stabilizations, some more clearly defined than others. As is only to be expected from museum material, precise geographical boundaries were impossible to draw and a great deal more information would be required to determine the circumstances in which one form of stabilization changes into another. In a wide southern belt on both sides of the Mediterranean spotting appears to have stabilized at levels quite unlike those of the greater part of Europe (the GE stabilization). Here, extensive samples showed that the insect achieved remarkable stability. But towards its periphery it tended towards increased variability in both sexes (see Fig. 17). Thus in the outlying populations of Ireland, Isles of Scilly, the Canary Islands, North Africa, and the three peninsulas of Iberia, Italy and Greece, also in the West Asian area, we find a

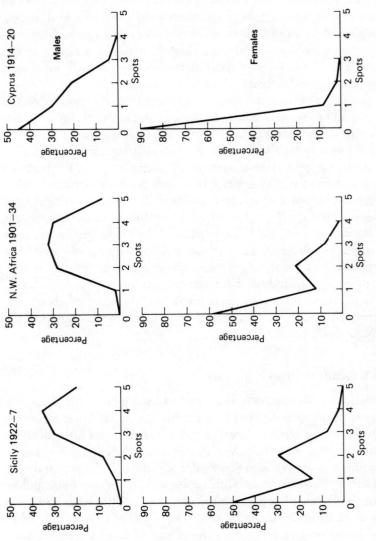

Figure 18 Some peripheral spot-stabilizations.

number of stabilizations each limited to a geographical area which is small compared with the GE zone. As was suggested in the previous chapter in connection with the transition from the SE to the EC and WC stabilizations, we would expect to find among specialized environments near the periphery of a species' distribution a range of ecological conditions to which it is not normally adjusted. These are just the circumstances in which we would anticipate unusual forms of variation to occur.

In Chapter 1 the point was made that patterns of spotting on the fore- and hind-wings similar to those found in the meadow brown are a universal feature of the family Satyridae and occur in several other butterfly families as well. This serves to underline the importance of the gene systems concerned, suggesting that the patterns of variation that they control may well be more significant than some of the other characters traditionally used in distinguishing species. Thus the West Asian (South) spot-distribution is apparent both in the meadow brown (*Maniola jurtina*) and in its near relative, *M. telmessia*; *M. cypricola* in Cyprus may provide another illustration of the same principle. In other words, the genes controlling spotting and its characteristic patterns appear to be trans-specific, trans-generic, trans-familial, and therefore of great antiquity. They may well have been established far longer than the genera and species existing today.

The meadow brown in Italy

A characteristic feature of the meadow brown in Britain is its long period of emergence. Thus in southern England the first males are usually on the wing in late June and fresh females are still to be found in late August, while in the Isles of Scilly the butterfly continues to fly well into September. On the hot plains of Italy the meadow brown is faced with ecological conditions quite unlike those in the more temperate parts of its range. Thus when sampling populations in Tuscany, Central Italy (Fig. 19), Dr Valerio Scali and his associates found that the period of emergence was quite short, lasting only 3–4 weeks, although it was longer (8–9 weeks) at altitudes of 300–700 m.[24, 25] After a few weeks at the peak of the summer all the meadow browns on the plains disappeared. Thereafter it was difficult to obtain a sample of either sex until September

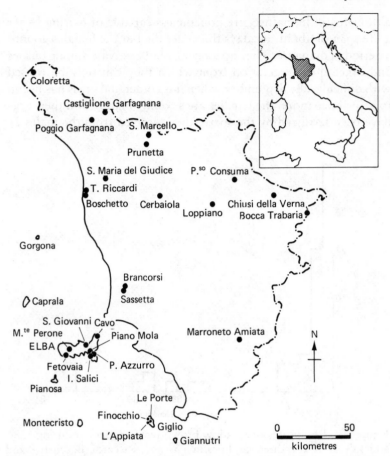

Figure 19 Map of Tuscany (Italy) showing sampling areas. The inset shows the position of Tuscany.

and then only females could be found. Two important questions followed: what had happened to the males, and were the females flying in September those which had flown earlier or ones that had emerged later? If the latter alternative were the case, it was difficult to see how fertilization could have occurred in the apparent absence of males.

Further studies in the field supported by laboratory investigations of the sequence of sexual development in the two sexes[26] revealed a remarkable state of affairs. At the time of their emergence from the pupa the males are sexually mature and the females, although still immature, are nonetheless capable of pairing. After a life span of about five days the males die but the females go into a period of diapause. They no longer fly but aestivate among bushes and other thick vegetation from which they can only be roused with difficulty. By September, when it is cooler and grass has begun to grow once more, the females are sexually mature and their eggs have been fertilized by the sperm they received from the males $2\frac{1}{2}$

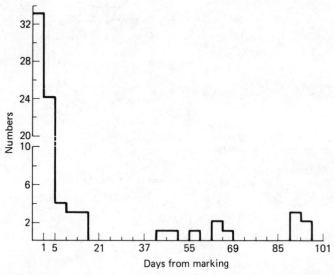

Figure 20   Recaptures of meadow brown females marked during June and July 1970–2 in three localities in Tuscany: Riccardi, Boschetto, and S. Maria del Giudice (see Fig. 19).

months earlier at the beginning of summer. Evidence that they were the same females which had flown before was derived from marking experiments and some typical results obtained by Scali are shown in Fig. 20. As a result of previous capture–recapture experiments it was known that the average life of a female meadow brown was about thirteen days.[11] The fact that recaptures of previously marked females extended over a period of 100 days provided convincing proof of aestivation.

A population of meadow browns at Prunetta (1000 m) presented a very different picture, as did another at 700 m. Here emergence began about a month later, no disappearance or even a temporary decrease in numbers being detectable throughout the summer. It was clear that no aestivation was occurring and that the situation was comparable with that in Britain, the only apparent difference being the period of emergence which was no more than about four weeks in Prunetta compared with the usual eight to nine in the Isles of Scilly.

Fortunately, Scali was able to find a population of meadow browns at an intermediate altitude at Poggio (430 m). No clear-cut gap occurred here between early and late individuals, but only a temporary reduction in numbers which was particularly marked at the end of July. At first sight it seemed that at this level no appreciable aestivation was occurring; however, the marking of females proved the contrary. Thus among the females flying in late August, some had been marked between 47–64 days earlier, showing that an appreciable period of diapause must have intervened. The capacity of the meadow brown to adjust the length of larval and pupal life to conform to the requirements of different ecological environments, shortening it in a hot climate where aestivation is necessary and lengthening it under more temperate conditions, provides a striking example of adaptation. Moreover, in achieving this both sexes play a part. Thus in a hot climate the males will have difficulty in obtaining the necessary liquid water from the environment and will have to rely largely on the oxidation of their fat, of which they have a relatively small amount. For them it is therefore a race against time and vital that pairing should take place quickly. The females have a far larger supply of fat and their capacity to survive at a low rate of metabolism is therefore greater. Their prime requirement is the availability of suitable vegetation for egg-laying which is only forthcoming once the hot season declines and the growth of grass begins again. The habit of aestivation is thus well designed to meet this need.

Summarizing the situation facing the meadow brown in Tuscany, it has been required to adapt to an extreme range of ecological conditions, from the heat of the plains to the cooler and more constant conditions at altitudes up to 1000 m. In achieving adjustment to both environments it has relied predominantly on two variables: the duration of larval and pupal development affecting the time and pattern of the emergence of adults, and delay in the achievement of female sexual maturity. At high altitudes such as Prunetta only the first is used; on the plains and offshore islands where it is hot, mainly the second method is employed; while at intermediate altitudes such as Poggio, both variables play an appreciable part.

Spot-distribution in Italy

Professor McWhirter's and my survey based on museum samples had shown that whatever the precise spot-distribution of meadow browns in the Central Mediterranean area might be, it appeared to diverge markedly from that of the GE stabilization in both sexes. However, the findings by Valerio Scali for populations in Tuscany did not support this view.[24] Indeed, a comparison of his samples with those in the British Museum from the south-east and south-west of the GE stabilization showed them to be similar ($P \simeq 0.7$ and $P > 0.2$ respectively).

But the most sensational findings concerned the pre-aestivation and post-aestivation females which exhibited marked intra-seasonal shift (see p. 70). Thus the pre-aestivation condition was a flat-topped spot-distribution with a mode at 1 and high values at 2 and 3 spots giving a spot average of 1.35. Post-aestivation, this distribution had changed to a large mode at 0 and a spot average of 0.91. Evidently, differential selection at a level calculated at 65 per cent had operated during the period of diapause against females with 2–5 spots. With high spotting at such a disadvantage at the end of the season, we may well ask why the genes causing it had not been eliminated long ago. The answer must be that a counterbalancing advantage exists for high spot-values during the early part of the season, and/or the genes for high spotting give an advantage to the early stages. Just what the nature of these advantages and disadvantages is we are not sure. By contrast, the male spot-distribution was unimodal at 2, closely resembling its GE counterpart. Since the life of the male is so short and it is not subject to aestivation like the female, it is hardly surprising to find no evidence of intra-seasonal variation.

Scali has also studied the meadow brown populations on the offshore islands of the Tuscan Archipalago,[27] Elba, Giglio, and Giannutri (for map see Fig. 19). The general picture is of a breakdown of the mainland stabilization comparable to that in the Isles of Scilly (see Chapter 5), each island assuming its own spot pattern. Of particular interest is the finding that this breakdown occurs not only in the females but in the males as well.

The sex ratio

In plants and animals which reproduce sexually, we tend to make the assumption that the two sexes occur in approximately equal numbers. Yet, quantitative evidence frequently proves the contrary. Thus in man the sex ratio at birth in England and Wales is 1.05 : 1 in favour of males; equality is reached between the ages of 15 and 19; while among those aged 85 and over there are twice as many women as there are men.

In the meadow brown, the kind of situation just described in the plain of Tuscany where adaptation to a period of intense heat is achieved through female aestivation, places additional pressure on the males to achieve fertilization over a limited period of a few weeks. As in Britain, the males invariably appear in July about a week before the females, thereby initiating an imbalance in the sex ratio. Moreover, the disappearance of the females at aestivation also has the effect of biasing samples in favour of males. However, Scali found that when both sexes were on the wing there was still a preponderance of males. Thus among pre-aestivation colonies on the Tuscan mainland during June and July the sex ratio ranged from 1.43 : 1 to 10.31 : 1 in favour of males, while on the island of Elba the ratios were more extreme (from 4.35–29.00 : 1).[28] The mountain colonies of Prunetta and Marcello in the north-west showed a similar preponderance of males in June and July, the sex ratio being gradually reversed in August until the males became non-existent by the end of the month.

Such a dynamic situation with important ecological implications for the survival of the insect in a diverse environment seemed worthy of further analysis. The evidence for varying sex ratios in the adults strongly suggested that powerful selection pressures could be at work controlling the sex-balance at different values in accordance with varying ecological requirements. But at what stages in the life cycle were these pressures at work? Were they only operational in the adult or was their effect more far-reaching, extending to the developmental stages as well? In attempting to answer these questions, Scali and Masetti decided to extend their studies to the eggs and larvae. This entailed

(a) obtaining a supply of eggs from wild females,
(b) rearing samples of larvae collected from populations where the sex ratios of the adults could also be determined,
(c) developing a reliable method of determining the sex of embryos and larvae.

Inducing female meadow browns to lay eggs in captivity caused no great difficulty since, given suitable conditions of temperature and light, they will lay readily on the sides of a cage lined with muslin. The technique had been evolved earlier in connection with other breeding experiments (to be considered further in Chapter 6). The same comments apply to the various larval stages, the second and third instar caterpillars being swept from grass by day, while the older larvae, which are nocturnal feeders, were swept at night. The sex both of the embryos developing from the fertilized eggs and the various larval stages had to be determined microscopically from squashes of dividing cells stained red with aceto-orcein. Female cells were easily distinguishable from male by the presence of a characteristic patch of sex chromatin (Plate 17).

Some typical results of these investigations are summarized in Table 15.

The distinction between the sex ratio of the embryos in favour of females and that of the later larval instars is striking. Moreover, if we add together the figures for larval instars 2, 3, and 4 and compare them with instar 5 we find that there is a significant difference $(P < 0.05)$.[27]

We are therefore faced with the extraordinary situation that in order to achieve the eventual sex ratio in the meadow brown

Table 15   Sex ratios in embryos and larvae from Il Boshetto (1972).

Date	Stage of development	Male	Female	Sex ratio
September 1972	Embryo	8	43	0.19
January–April 1972	Larva instars 2–3	13	16	0.81
April–May 1972	Larva instar 4	39	49	0.80
April–May 1972	Larva instar 5	109	83	1.31

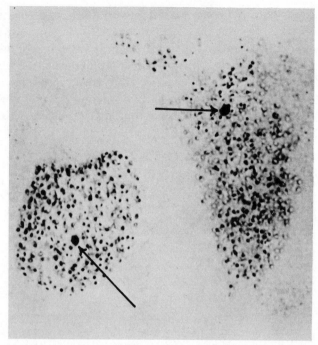

a

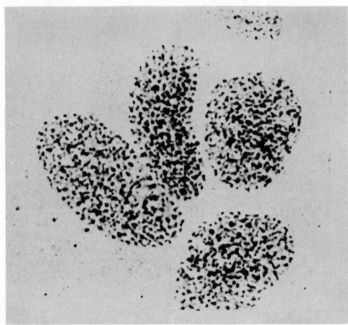

b

Plate 17 (a) Female cells from a fifth instar larva showing the sex chromatin (arrowed); (b) male fifth instar cells with no sex chromatin. (×1500).

populations on the Tuscan plains, powerful selective elimination of males takes place at the embryo stage; this is continued in the early larval instars, but in lesser degree; and by the time of the final instar selection is in the opposite direction favouring the survival of males, a situation which, as we have seen, continues in the adults. Such a process where selection operates in one direction during the young stages and in another later on has been termed endocyclic selection.

5

𝓑𝓑𝓑𝓑𝓑𝓑𝓑𝓑𝓑𝓑𝓑𝓑𝓑𝓑𝓑𝓑𝓑𝓑𝓑𝓑𝓑𝓑

Studying island populations

Because of their isolation, islands can provide outdoor laboratories for the study of evolution. The powerful effects of geographical barriers such as the sea in promoting diversity among island populations of animals and plants was realised by naturalists early last century. Thus, on visiting the Galapagos archipelago in 1835, Darwin recorded that of the twenty-six species of land birds he observed, at least twenty-one were peculiar to the islands. By contrast, of the eleven species of marine birds, with their greater mobility, only two were unknown elsewhere.[29]

As far as the meadow brown is concerned we have seen how isolation, both at local and continental levels, has had profound effects on spot-distribution. Indeed, it was in an island context that spotting was first discovered to be a variant which could be used as a parameter for measuring the effects of selection. Following this early discovery we asked ourselves a number of questions. In the light of the marked differences existing between the butterfly populations on Tean in the Isles of Scilly and those of the Cornish peninsula (particularly the females) could it be that the colonists of the other islands also differed from the mainland and, possibly, from one another? Was the situation of the meadow brown in Scilly comparable to that of the birds in the Galapagos? Lack visited the islands in 1939 and found not only that there were unique species, as Darwin had described, but that some, such as the finches, had evolved races peculiar to each island.[30] Again, if such insular variations occurred, did these represent stabilizations, as on the mainland, or were they of a more fluctuating kind? Early work on Tean had shown us that, just as a gap of sea of a few hundred metres provided a barrier to meadow brown movement, so too could a strip of windswept ground effectively isolate one population of butterflies from another. In these circumstances was it possible that localized races could be formed—islands within islands, so to speak? Such questions, first formulated in 1938, and others deriving from them played an important part in shaping our researches in the Isles of Scilly, which began in 1946 and are still continuing. It is with these that this chapter will be concerned.

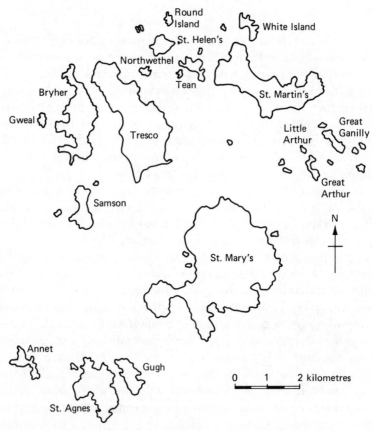

Figure 21   The Isles of Scilly (smallest islands omitted).

The Isles of Scilly form an archipelago situated some 48 km west-south-west of Land's End, Cornwall. Some of the islands are quite large (five are inhabited) while others are little more than rocks, the majority being arranged roughly round a shallow central road-stead about 4 km by 3 km in extent (Fig. 21). For our studies of the meadow brown we divided the islands into two groups—the large islands of St Mary's, Tresco, and St Martin's with areas of 280 hectares or more, and the small ones of 16 hectares or less, representing a difference in area of at least 17 times.

The large islands

Apart from small changes due to building, the ecology of St Mary's has remained relatively unchanged since we first collected there in 1951. The island is by far the largest and includes a wide variety of terrain including cultivated fields, rough grassland, bracken, and

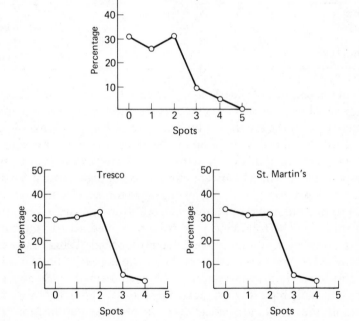

Figure 22 Spot-distribution of meadow brown females on the three large islands of Scilly.

heath. Consistent sampling of the meadow brown population over a period of nine years revealed a remarkable stability in spot-distribution.[31] Thus the males, in general, showed their characteristic mode at 2 spots, while in the females spotting had stabilized at a curious flat-topped level with approximately equal values at 0, 1, and 2 (see Fig. 22). On Tresco (the second largest island) spotting was similar to that on St Mary's until 1957. That year we witnessed one of the greatest ecological changes ever seen in the Isles of Scilly. A prolonged drought during May and June, a critical period in the development of the meadow brown, resulted in a massive reduction of the grass, inroads by bramble and bracken, and a great increase in the area occupied by the hottentot fig (*Carpobrotus edulis*), a

Table 16   Spot-distribution of female meadow browns on Tresco (main area) 1950-9.

| Date | Spots | | | | | | | Spot average |
	0	1	2	3	4	5	Total	
1950–56	174	166	185	31	10	1	567	1.19
1957	21	17	8	2	–	–	48	0.81
1958	23	41	32	13	6	–	115	1.46
1959	10	10	8	1	–	–	29	1.00

common colonist of the islands, particularly in areas bordering the sea. Small wonder that in such circumstances there was a marked fluctuation in the number of butterflies, as the small sample shown in Table 16 indicates. Although we shall never know for certain, it seems likely that this combination of adverse circumstances was responsible for the 61 per cent elimination of high-spotted females that took place in 1957,[31] converting a flat-topped distribution (Fig. 22) to one unimodal at 0, and the spot average from 1.19 to 0.81 (Table 16). The following year conditions had greatly improved and population numbers were nearer normal. Female spotting appeared to 'over-correct' after the previous year's elimination of high-spotted individuals and now showed a small mode at 1 and the unusually high spot average of 1.46. In 1959, judging by a small sample, the population had achieved its previous stabilization once more (Table 16).

By comparison with Tresco, the ecological changes observed on

St Martin's, the third of the large islands we studied, were comparatively small. However, there was also a clear trend towards a reduction in the area of grassland with corresponding inroads of bracken and bramble. The effects of drought were clearly evident in 1957 and a reduction in numbers followed. Like the other large islands, spot-distribution had remained stable for the six-year period 1950–5 (Fig. 22). But in 1956 and 1957 (Table 17) the same signs were apparent as on Tresco, namely a heavy elimination of high-spotted females resulting in an excess at 0 and a corresponding reduction in spot average, which was no doubt a response to similar ecological pressures. But unlike Tresco, the return to the characteristic flat-topped distribution was more fluctuating, being achieved in 1958 but showing a reduced trend towards low-spotting in 1959 (Table 17).

Table 17 Spot-distribution in female meadow browns on St Martin's (main area) 1950–9.

Date	Spots						Total	Spot average
	0	1	2	3	4	5		
1950–5	272	251	247	41	15	–	826	1.12
1956	63	49	43	6	–	–	161	0.95
1957	73	42	42	10	–	–	167	0.93
1958	46	43	43	15	6	1	154	1.32
1959	36	23	22	3	–	–	84	0.91

The picture of spot-variation in the meadow brown populations on the three large islands is thus of a basic stabilization with occasional fluctuations at second order level. In the males, the spot pattern has never deviated from the characteristic unimodal distribution at 2. Curiously, when deviations towards reduced spotting occurred in the females, as on Tresco and St Martin's in 1957, the tendency among the males was to move in the opposite direction towards slightly higher spot-values. Among the females, marked changes occurred from 1957 onwards, high spotting being at a strong selective disadvantage. But as ecological conditions improved the previous situation tended to be restored, sometimes, as on Tresco, in a single generation.

St Martin's—a more detailed analysis

In our studies of meadow brown populations on the English mainland described in Chapter 3, we seldom encountered a flat-topped distribution at 0, 1, and 2 spots in the females as we had found so consistently on the three large islands in Scilly. Where it occurred it invariably indicated either a transitional zone between bimodality and unimodality, or a population in the process of changing from one form of spotting to another in response to a varying environment. The situation on St Mary's, St Martin's, and Tresco seemed so peculiar that we felt it justified a more detailed analysis.

When describing the three islands it was emphasized that their terrain was diverse, ranging from grassland, both rough and cultivated, to bramble thickets, bracken, heathland, and even large areas of *Carpobrotus*. In obtaining samples of butterflies each year we had taken care always to collect them from the same areas. Even so, the localities visited fluctuated considerably in their ecology. Could it be that the flat-topped female spot-distributions were really the additive effect of sampling a number of different populations? Admittedly, the likelihood of repeating the error so faithfully in three different places was somewhat remote, nonetheless we were aware that at the extremity of its range the butterfly was more than usually sensitive to environmental influences and therefore could be capable of response by evolving a mosaic of localized races.

St Martin's seemed the obvious island to choose for this analysis, partly because it was the smallest of the 'large' islands and the most easily workable, and also because we knew it best. Moreover, it was easily accessible from the neighbouring island of Tean where our camp was located. Accordingly, we identified 10 different sampling areas (Fig. 23) each characterized by a particular topography and vegetation.[31, 32] The main sample each year had been collected from sub-areas B and C (see Fig. 23) and over a period of three years (1977-9) these proved to be completely homogeneous.

At the extremity of its range, as we have seen, the meadow brown becomes increasingly sensitive to its environment, populations occupying isolated areas adjusting to the special conditions of their habitats. It was therefore of some interest to discover the types of spotting characteristic of populations in small ecological

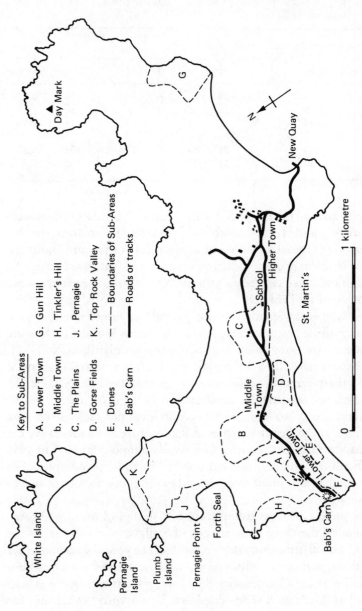

Figure 23 St Martin's and White Island showing the boundaries of the sampling areas.

Key to Sub-Areas

A. Lower Town
b. Middle Town
C. The Plains
D. Gorse Fields
E. Dunes
F. Bab's Carn
G. Gun Hill
H. Tinkler's Hill
J. Pernagie
K. Top Rock Valley
--- Boundaries of Sub-Areas
━━━ Roads or tracks

White Island

Pernagie Island

Plumb Island

Pernagie Point

Forth Seal

Bab's Carn

Day Mark

Gun Hill

New Quay

School

Higher Town

St. Martin's

Middle Town

Lower Town

0   1 kilometre

Table 18   Spot-distribution of female meadow browns in two isolated populations on St Martin's.

		Spots							Spot
Sub-area	Date	0	1	2	3	4	5	Total	average
G	1953	55	24	27	4	–	–	110	0.82
	1958	17	21	16	2	–	–	56	1.05
	1959	26	12	5	1	–	–	44	0.57
H	1953	51	21	24	7	–	–	103	0.87
	1958	44	25	24	7	–	–	100	0.94

enclaves around the periphery of the island. Typical examples were sub-areas G and H, each of which appeared to be isolated from the main body of the island either by areas of cultivation and buildings, or by particular geographical and vegetational features. The results of sampling these two populations over a span of seven years are summarized in Table 18.

The figures for female spotting provide an interesting comparison with those from the main area (sub-areas B and C), showing a tendency to move away from a flat-topped distribution at 0, 1, and 2 spots towards a unimodal distribution at 0, reminiscent of the Southern English stabilization on the mainland (see Chapter 3). Although not statistically significant from the main area ($P > 0.2$), the trend proved to be more marked in localities such as sub-area K, where the difference achieved significance.[32] Incidentally, the curious deviation in sub-area G towards unimodality at 1 in 1958 is difficult to explain in the light of earlier and later samples. The total number was small so this could have represented error due to sampling.

The picture thus emerging from our studies of meadow brown spotting on the three large islands of Scilly was as follows. In the males, spot-distribution, although subject to periodic second order variations, invariably followed the well established pattern of unimodality at 2. In the females the basic spot-distribution was flat-topped at 0, 1, and 2, with occasional second order variations; for instance, that on Tresco in 1958 which showed a mode at 1. Detailed investigations on St Martin's showed that the flat-topped pattern was indeed a genuine stabilization and not just an amalgam of a number of separate populations. However, in isolated areas, pockets of variation had built up which were stable from year to year and distinct from the main island form.

The small islands

By contrast with the large islands of Scilly and their wide diversity of terrain, the ecology of each of the small islands is highly specific. Thus they differ markedly from one another not only in the habitats they provide but also in their aspect relative to wind, temperature, and rainfall. Like the large islands, we obtained samples of meadow browns from the small islands spanning the period 1946–59, involving fourteen generations of the butterfly. Here again we found remarkable stability, but while the males everywhere exhibited the expected mode at 2 spots, the females had evidently achieved a range of different stabilizations, each one specific to a particular island (Fig. 24). In this respect, the meadow browns on the Isles of Scilly show a striking parallel with the finches of the Galapagos Islands (p. 93). Indeed, the scene in Scilly is in one sense the more interesting, because here we are faced with the unique situation that while female spotting on the large islands is basically similar, that on the small islands is different. This illustrates beautifully an important biological principle, namely that populations occupying small restricted habitats adapt independently to each set of differing ecological situations, but when spread over a larger and more diverse area they adjust to the average of the conditions that exist there.

The evolution of island stabilizations

Faced with the situation outlined above, we spent much time discussing possible mechanisms by which it could have come about. So, too, did other biologists working in this field, both in Britain and abroad. A number of possible explanations were forthcoming.

(a) Could it be that the butterflies resembled one another on the large islands but not on the small ones because of migration between them? In such circumstances, the likelihood of new colonists reaching small islands would be far less than for large

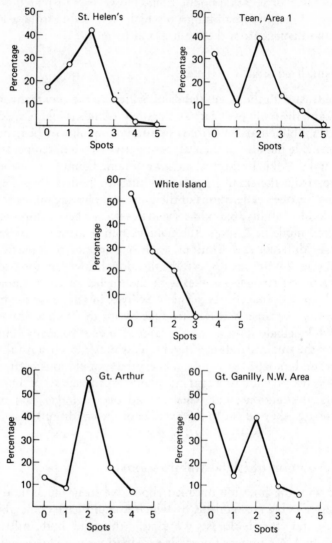

Figure 24 Spot-distribution of female meadow browns on five small islands of Scilly; that on White Island is before 1958.

islands and this could lead to the observed differences. Such a view is largely untenable in the light of three pieces of evidence. First, extensive marking experiments on Tean and St Martin's had shown that migration between them was a rare event. Second, our studies on Tean in Areas 3 and 5 (see Fig. 4) had shown that 100 m of windswept ground provided an almost complete barrier to butterfly movement. Lastly, there was the situation just described which provided the most powerful evidence of all, in which small islands lying quite close together differed radically from one another in their female meadow brown spot-distributions. There were thus ample grounds for rejecting a migration hypothesis.

(b) An alternative explanation invoked the influence of 'genetic drift', which depends upon the random distribution of genes in populations whose numbers are small. Ford[22] has explained the situation neatly as follows. Suppose two genes A and a occur in a population with a frequency of 50 per cent, that is to say in a 1 : 1 ratio. If we disregard any effects of selection or survival, then in theory we might expect the ratio to be maintained in the next generation. But in practice this does not happen due to the effects of chance on the gene combinations coming together at fertilization. Thus in a population of say 500 individuals, where $A + a$ therefore total 1000, the ratio of $A : a$ might well be 498 : 502. Here, the incidence of a exceeds expectation by 0.4 per cent. But suppose we have a small population of only 10 individuals and a similar excess of a giving a ratio $A : a$ of 8 : 12. Now a will exceed expectation by 20 per cent, and in the next generation there will be only two-thirds as many gametes carrying A as there are of a. Sometimes the effect of chance may be towards restoring the original ratio, at other times the disparity may be further enhanced. Genetic drift, although a mathematical certainty, exerts an appreciable effect only in small populations. But even then, to be effective it will have to outweigh the effects of selection which, as we have seen, can be exceedingly powerful.

Returning to the Isles of Scilly, we already possessed two important pieces of evidence enabling us to determine the likelihood that genetic drift could have played an appreciable part in bringing about the situation on the large and small islands. The use of the mark–release–recapture method for estimating population numbers (see Chapter 2) had provided us with information on the size of the butterfly populations occupying the three areas of Tean. These totalled approximately 15 000, 3000, and 500 individuals.[11] An estimate of the numbers on St Helen's to the north-west of Tean (Fig. 21), one of the small islands (see Fig. 24), suggested a figure of around 15 000–20 000 insects. Such populations were far in excess of those likely to exhibit the random effects of genetic drift. The second relevant type of evidence derives from our estimates of selection pressures, for instance, the elimination of 61 per cent of the high-spotted females among the main Tresco colony in 1957. As studies of the boundary phenomenon on the mainland had shown (Chapter 3), such pressures were to be regarded now as the rule rather than the exception. Clearly, they were of a different order of magnitude from any effect that could possibly accrue through random genetic drift.

(c) A further explanation of island spotting was based on the occurrence of periodic fluctuations in population numbers and the possibility that increases taking place over a period of years had enabled new gene combinations to be established as in the colony of the marsh fritillary *Euphydryas* (*Melitaea*) *aurinia* studied by H. D. and E. B. Ford.[7] The objection to this hypothesis was that with the exception of rare fluctuations in numbers or of extreme climatic variations such as occurred in 1957, the size of the populations of meadow browns both on the large and small islands seemed to have remained remarkably constant.

(d) The 'founder principle' elaborated by Mayr[33] has also been invoked to explain the diversity of spot-stabilizations, particularly on the small islands. This rests on the assumption that at various times in the past the different islands were colonized either by odd migrants from elsewhere or by the remaining few individuals that survived a severe fluctuation in numbers. The theory left much to speculation and, as the foregoing account has shown, it did not concur with the facts, such as the sensitivity of populations to changing environmental conditions as evidenced by their varying spot-values.

(e) Another aspect of (c) above, was the idea of 'intermittent drift' suggested by Waddington.[34] This envisaged a situation in which a population reached, either through fluctuation or a slow build-up of numbers from a few founders, a density low enough for random genetic drift to exert an appreciable effect over a period of time. This might explain the diversity of spotting on the small islands. That the large islands, by contrast, exhibited such homogeneity was presumably accounted for by assuming that even when numbers of butterflies were at a minimum there were still sufficient to mask the effects of drift. As with the previous suggestions, the problem here was to reconcile theory with the established facts, particularly those relating to observed changes in spot-distribution.

In the light of previous experience our inclination was to discard all five propositions in favour of an explanation based on selection. Three important pieces of evidence derived from the islands of Tean, White Island, and Great Ganilly (see Fig. 21), strongly supported a selectionist viewpoint.

Selection on three small islands

(a) TEAN

Reference has already been made in Chapter 2 to our early experiences on the small uninhabited island of Tean, particularly the development of a procedure of mark–release–recapture for the estimation of the size of meadow brown populations. One of the most powerful factors controlling the ecology of the island was a herd of cattle which closely grazed such grassland as existed, particularly in Areas 2 and 4 (Fig. 25). The result was two lawn-like stretches of grass 180 m and 130 m long respectively. Both were completely windswept and, as observation and marking experiments showed, were virtually total barriers to butterfly movement. Any insects attempting to cross them either turned back or were blown out to sea. In the autumn of 1950 the cattle were removed permanently. At first the effect of the reduction in grazing pressure was hardly noticeable but by 1953 the growth of grass had achieved almost hayfield proportions. Butterflies could frequently be seen moving unimpeded from Area 1 into Area 2 and from Area 5 into Area 4. Area 3 was now the only major ecological barrier on the

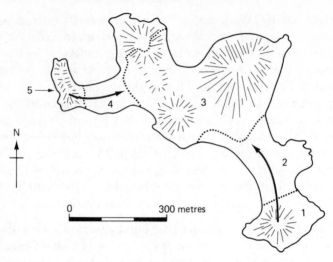

Figure 25   Map of Tean (Isles of Scilly) showing the directions of colonization after the removal of cattle in the autumn of 1950.

island holding apart the populations of meadow browns inhabiting the southern limb (Areas 1 and 2) and the western limb (Areas 4 and 5). Sampling these populations in 1953 and again in 1954 showed that in Areas 1 and 2 female spotting had remained unaltered ($P > 0.2$).[31, 35, 36] However, that in Areas 4 and 5 had changed completely, being bimodal in 1953 but becoming unimodal at 2 in 1954 ($P < 0.05$). The situation is shown graphically in Fig. 26. In order to achieve this change there must have been selection of some 64 per cent against unspotted females in 1954. It should be noted that the new spot-value in the population of the western limb then stabilized, remaining constant in subsequent years.

The ecological changes on Tean between 1950 and 1954, and the adjustment of the meadow brown to them as evidenced by changes in female spotting, posed an interesting problem. Why did an extension of range have such a profound effect on one community and not on the other? A possible explanation is that the population of Area 1 had spread across Area 2 without adjusting its spot-frequency because the ecology of the two places had become very similar. Not only had the grass grown, but bracken had encroached across most of Area 2, thus affording the same degree of shelter

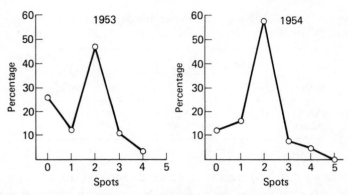

Figure 26 Spot-distribution of female meadow browns in the western section of Tean (Isles of Scilly) showing the change associated with altered ecology between 1953 and 1954.

that had always been available to the butterfly in Area 1. However, the population in Area 5 had spread eastwards into Area 4 although it differed from it greatly, colonization being possible only because of the growth of long grass. The sheltering bracken so characteristic of Areas 1, 2 and 5 was absent from Area 4, creating ecological conditions unlike those occurring anywhere else on the island. The single population now inhabiting Areas 4 and 5 combined had thus had to adjust to the average of the peculiar ecological conditions prevailing there, resulting in a different spot-distribution from any previously recorded on Tean. By contrast, in Area 2 where a mixture of long grass and bracken prevailed, the meadow brown population had retained its familiar characteristics.

(b) WHITE ISLAND
This island is situated to the north of St Martin's (Fig. 23) and connected by a tumble of seaweed-covered rocks 200 m long, exposed at about half tide. Bearing in mind the evidence provided by Area 4 on Tean, it seemed likely that the population of meadow browns inhabiting White Island would be quite isolated. The area of the island is about 16 hectares so it falls within the small-island group of Scilly.[36] The first samples were obtained in 1953, and from then until 1957 female spotting was stable with a high mode at 0 (spot average 0.68). During the winter of 1957–8 storms penetrated the isthmus separating the north and south portions of the island,

Table 19   Spot-distributions of female meadow browns on the two parts of White Island, Isles of Scilly, 1958–68.

| | Spots | | | | | Spot |
Area	0	1	2	3+	Total	average
North	317	164	87	10	578	0.64
South	147	148	140	25	460	1.09

obliterating a belt of vegetation-covered sand and stones and leaving a gap about 30 m wide. From our previous experience we realized that this might now constitute a partial barrier to meadow brown movement so from 1958 we sampled the two halves of the island separately. Our predictions proved justified for the two populations now became strikingly distinct, that in the north assuming a female spot average of 0.64 while in the south it increased to 1.09 ($P < 0.001$). The relevant data are summarized in Table 19 and shown graphically in Fig. 27.

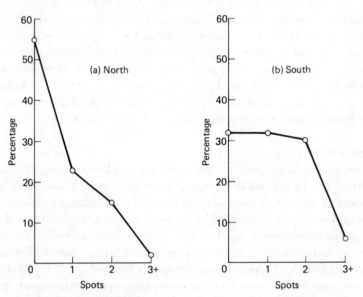

Figure 27   Female spot-distributions on the two parts of White Island (Isles of Scilly), 1958–68.

Thereafter the situation stabilized for a period of 11 years. By 1969, in the absence of further severe storms, the barrier created in 1957-8 had been largely obliterated by the recolonization of plants across it.[31, 32] Samples of females collected in 1969-71 are summarized in Table 20.

The spot averages suggest that the insects on the northern part of the island tended to remain at the spot-level current prior to 1958. Those in the south, having diverged to such a marked degree, evidently returned to the original pattern, achieving homogeneity

Table 20 Samples of female meadow browns on the two parts of White Island 1969-71.

	Spots							Spot average
	0	1	2	3	4	5	Total	
North								
1969	15	9	4	1	–	–	29	0.69
1970	17	13	9	1	2	–	42	1.00
1971	19	9	5	–	–	–	33	0.58
South								
1969	15	6	4	–	–	–	25	0.56
1970	16	15	7	1	2	–	41	0.98
1971	13	5	5	–	–	–	23	0.65

within the island once more $(P > 0.9)$. A comparison of the new spotting with that existing in 1953-7 shows them to be similar $(P = 0.7)$. Precisely why one part of the island should have diverged during a period when the other remained unchanged is not clear, but presumably this was associated with the varying microclimates characterizing the two habitats, which faced in different directions. It should be added that throughout the period of study the male samples tended to be small partly on account of the difficulty in catching the more agile insect in such an exposed place and also because, by the time we reached the island, the population of males (which emerged before the females) was already becoming depleted. However, where the samples were large enough, they tended to conform to the pattern of change in the females.

(c) GREAT GANILLY

This is another uninhabited island about the same size as White Island and situated among the Eastern Isles to the south-east of St Martin's (see Fig. 21). Its overall length is about 80 m and it consists essentially of two low hills joined by a sandy isthmus about 50 m wide. When first sampled in 1951 and 1955 the males exhibited the typical unimodal 2-spot condition. But from 1956 onwards they showed a tendency towards unimodality at 3 or 4 spots—a situation unique in our experience of populations in Britain. In 1958, following the studies on White Island described above, we decided that it might be advisable to collect the north and south portions of the island separately. The male samples from 1961–8 proved homogeneous and are summarized in Table 21.

Table 21   Spot-distribution in meadow browns on Great Ganilly 1961–8.

	Spots							Spot average
	0	1	2	3	4	5	Total	
Males								
North	–	1	37	48	63	7	156	3.24
South	–	–	34	83	76	18	211	3.37
Females								
North	63	39	127	40	9	4	282	1.66
South	54	44	143	62	7	2	312	1.78

The difference between the two populations is not quite significant ($P < 0.10$) but the general trend is clear enough.[22] As might be expected, the situation in the females was more extreme. In 1958 the population of the northern sector was bimodal at 0 and 2 spots while the southern was unimodal at 2 with low and nearly equal values at 0 and 1. From 1961–8 the position evidently stabilized and the samples obtained over this period proved to be homogeneous (see Table 21). Although the difference was now less extreme in that both populations had tended towards bimodality, nonetheless there is a significant difference between them ($P < 0.01$).[22] As on White Island, the butterfly had evidently adjusted differentially to two sets of somewhat differing environmental conditions, the isthmus of 50 m constituting an effective barrier between the two populations. But there is an added interest attaching to the situation on Great Ganilly in that adjustment took place in both sexes, not in the female alone.

On Tean, White Island, and Great Ganilly we thus have three populations of meadow browns that reacted to environmental change by assuming new spot-distributions. In no instance were the populations concerned subject to large fluctuations in numbers or so small as to suggest that 'founders' or 'intermittent drift' were playing an appreciable part in bringing such changes about. On the contrary, we were able on occasions, as on Tean where the influence of cattle was so marked, to identify with some degree of certainty the nature of the ecological conditions promoting change—a fact which strengthens still further an explanation based on the influence of selection.

When interpreting the results of our work in the meadow brown in the Scillies and elsewhere, there is a danger of adopting a viewpoint which is too facile and generalized to account for the relatively complex situations described in the previous pages. Typical of such misunderstandings is the account by Shorrocks.[37] Thus he states that on the large islands the female spot-distributions remained constant from year to year. In fact there were fluctuations on occasions as in the Tresco population in 1957 (p. 96) correlated with drastic changes in the environment. The important point here is that after such changes, spotting returned to its former pattern of large island stabilization. He also assumes that the large islands with their diversity of terrain represent the sum of the conditions on the small islands. This is certainly not so. In fact, as has been emphasized earlier, each small island possesses an ecology peculiar to its particular topography and isolation. Moreover, far from being uniform as Shorrocks supposes, their environment can be highly heterogeneous as is evidenced by our studies on Tean, White Island, and Great Ganilly (pp. 105–10) where spot-distributions in the meadow brown responded sensitively to identifiable environmental variations.

The Tresco Farm Area

The populations of meadow browns described so far were all relatively large and therefore not of a kind that would be expected to exhibit the effects of 'genetic drift' or of 'founders'. But bearing in mind the effectiveness of small ecological barriers in isolating portions of populations, it would have been surprising if, in remote, peripheral areas, there had not occurred colonies of a size which might be expected to show the effects of random gene survival. Just such a colony occurred in a small enclave of about 180 m × 65 m, isolated from the Main Area of Tresco and occupying an entirely abnormal habitat immediately south of the farm buildings at New Grimsby. A number of huts had been erected there during the 1914–18 war and around their concrete foundations had grown up a dense vegetation quite peculiar to the island, consisting largely of escapes from cultivation. The population of meadow browns occupying this specialized habitat was almost completely isolated from the Main Area by pastureland, bramble, and scrub. A path connected the two localities and it is possible that a few insects migrated along it, although none was seen doing so even where the density was high. An estimate of population size was made by the mark–release–recapture method which showed that the daily flying population of meadow browns in the Farm Area was of the order of 100–150 insects.[36] There was thus a possibility that these numbers would be small enough to reveal the effects of genetic drift.

Table 22   Spot-distributions in female meadow brown populations of the Farm and Main Areas of Tresco 1954-6.

| | Spots | | | | | | | Spot |
	0	1	2	3	4	5	Total	average
Farm Area								
1954	5	6	18	6	–	–	35	1.71
1955	23	16	40	6	4	–	89	1.46
1956	6	11	15	3	1	–	36	1.50
Total	34	33	73	15	5	–	160	1.53
Main Area								
1954	26	28	36	5	1	–	96	1.24
1955	32	31	27	7	4	–	101	1.21
1956	34	30	34	5	2	–	105	1.15
Total	92	89	97	17	7	–	302	1.20

Sampling over the three years 1954–6 showed the characteristic female spot-distribution in the Farm Area to have remained unchanged (Table 22; $P > 0.5$).

It will be noted from Table 22 that female spotting in the Farm Area judged by spot average was different from that of the population in the Main Area of Tresco. The difference is reinforced by a formal test of significance ($P < 0.01$) indicating the degree of isolation of the smaller colony. The drought of 1957 which decimated the meadow brown population on the Main Area of Tresco almost depopulated the Farm Area. Thus a search involving four net-hours at the height of the season produced only four butterflies, all females. Here, indeed, was a situation in which the operation of random genetic drift or the founder principle might have been expected to be decisive in controlling the evolution of the Farm Area colony once numbers began to increase. This they did the following year (1958) by which time the vegetation had largely recovered. Yet, after extreme numerical depletion, we found that the female population had returned to the same exceptional female spot-frequency (unimodal at 2) that had obtained previously (see Table 22). A comparison between the population of 1958 and that of 1954–6 gives $P > 0.3$, indicating a close similarity between them. That this return to a previous spot value by the Farm Area population is not explicable in terms of migration is indicated by the fact that spot-distribution in the Main Area, from which any migrants would have come, was known throughout the whole period. It was never of the kind found in the Farm Area.

Thus it is clear that any effects that founders or drift might have exerted under conditions of low population density were masked by powerful selection in favour of a type adapted to the abnormal conditions prevailing in the habitat.

Establishing experimental populations

The existence of characteristic spot-stabilizations among the meadow brown populations of the large and small islands, also the occurrence of discrete isolated colonies within islands, are in accord with a view of evolutionary adjustment under the influence of powerful selective forces to a diverse range of ecological conditions. As Ford has pointed out,[22] we have never yet encountered a situation in one of these restricted habitats where the meadow brown population has exhibited the large island type of spot-distribution. A single exception was on White Island South (1958–68) but this differed significantly from the colony on the nearest part of St Martin's opposite. Under exceptional conditions of ecological change (drought) the butterflies on St Martin's and Tresco temporarily assumed a new type of spotting, only to return to the former pattern later. By contrast the large island of St Mary's remained unaffected, presumably because it was able to provide a greater diversity of ecological alternatives than the others.

It occurred to us that if we could establish on a small island a population of meadow browns with a large island spot-distribution, it might be possible to subject our ideas to experimental test using rigorous quantitative methods. Accordingly, in 1953 we set about prospecting for suitable islands. To meet our requirements we needed one or more which

(a) were reasonably accessible under varying conditions of weather and tide,
(b) did not already support a meadow brown population,
(c) were ecologically suitable for the establishment of a colony of butterflies.

The Eastern Isles (Fig. 21) seemed to provide the most likely possibilities, and after a considerable search we selected two of them, Menawethan and Great Innisvowles, for our experimental colonies. These islands were much the same size with a circumference of around 200 m. Menawethan was covered in a dense growth of grass and no bracken. One of the commonest flowering plants growing in huge tufts was birdsfoot trefoil (*Lotus corniculatus*) which supported a flourishing population of the common blue (*Polyommatus icarus*). The meadow brown was evidently absent. Great Innisvowles was more diverse with grass, bramble and some bracken. By contrast with Menawethan, collecting was relatively easy. Again, there was a flourishing colony of common blues but no meadow browns.

The following summer we collected a large sample on the Main Area of St Martin's (which also provided a control) and liberated 120 females on Menawethan and 117 on Great Innisvowles. In releasing only females we assumed that the majority had already paired almost immediately after emergence, as normally occurs. On visiting Menawethan in 1955 it was soon clear that the population was hanging on precariously. Two days' collecting yielded altogether 18 insects, 7 males and 11 females (spot average 0.91). In addition, 8 butterflies caught and marked on the first occasion were recaught on the second, suggesting that the population at that time was probably not more than 20. Accordingly, we augmented it with a further 124 females from St Martin's (spot average 1.27). The experimental population on Great Innisvowles had fared little better and mark–release–recapture data suggested a total of about 30. These included 17 females with a spot average of 1.44. The following summer a visit to Menawethan in good collecting weather indicated that the population was almost extinct, a day's collecting producing only two insects. Taking into account the difficulty of landing on the island which was only possible in fine weather and at a relatively high tide, also the limited suitability of the habitat for colonization by meadow browns, we decided reluctantly to abandon Menawethan and to concentrate our efforts on Great Innisvowles. Here the situation was little better and exhaustive collecting produced only 3 butterflies, all females. We therefore decided to augment the colony with a further 106 females from St Martin's (spot average 0.96). The following summer (1957) the colony appeared to be on the verge of extinction, only three insects being caught, but by 1958 it had recovered a little, yielding a total of 15, including 11 females with a spot average of 1.27. The comparable figure for the Main Area of St Martin's that year was 1.24. Thereafter, the Great Innisvowles colony continued to survive precariously at a low ebb until last visited in 1964 when only a single male was observed.

The results of establishing experimental meadow brown populations on Menawethan and Great Innisvowles must therefore be judged inconclusive. In so far as our limited results go, these seemed to indicate a trend in the Menawethan population towards a decreasing spot average compared with the Main Area of St Martin's, while that on Great Innisvowles showed a movement in the reverse direction towards an increased spot average. However, neither difference was statistically significant. Why neither experimental population succeeded in establishing itself is difficult to say. The exposure of both islands to strong winds and a lack of suitable shelter must have played a part; so, too, must the general micro-ecology of the terrain. One other observation of ours may have been significant. Evidently, both islands supported a flourishing colony of wrens—an insectivorous species, and we noticed that the birds frequently positioned themselves where they could observe the numerous plants of ragwort (*Senecio jacobaea*) whose flowers were attractive to meadow browns, particularly females. On Great Innisvowles in particular, we noted a number of instances of damaged wings indicating attempted bird predation, although we never actually witnessed an attack on either sex. However, this did occur on the small copper (*Lycaena phlaeas*), indicating that butterflies were certainly part of the birds' diet, to which our experimental populations of meadow browns may well have contributed an all too welcome addition!

6

╚╚╚╚╚╚╚╚╚╚╚╚╚╚╚╚╚╚╚╚╚╚╚╚╚╚╚

The significance of spotting

Our studies of the meadow brown in such diverse circumstances as the European continent, the English mainland, and the Isles of Scilly have demonstrated beyond doubt that hind-wing spotting can provide a sensitive index both of population stability and of change. Moreover, the use of this parameter in the context of widespread field studies has thrown considerable light on the circumstances in which stabilization and microevolution are achieved in a variety of different ecological situations. Yet a curious paradox remained. In spite of the successful use of spot-distribution, spot-placing and spot average as measures of adaptive change, we still had little idea of the significance for the individual butterfly of the presence or absence of spots and their numerical porportions. Our attempts to throw some light on this problem from a number of different viewpoints are the subject of this chapter.

The work on the meadow brown illustrates beautifully the inherent limitations of fieldwork as an investigatory technique. While this can be highly effective in isolating and defining problems, also in monitoring situations, it is generally of limited value in elucidating the precise nature of adaptive mechanisms. By their very nature these are ultimately physiological, and their investigation demands a level of rigour and control such as is usually impossible in the field. Sooner or later the problem must be transferred to the laboratory.

Having reached this point we asked ourselves a number of questions, for instance,

1. To what extent can spotting be related to adult survival?
2. Can there be any relationship between adult spotting and selective advantage or disadvantage during the earlier phases of the life cycle?
3. Can spot-change, such as occurred in the boundary area (see Chapter 3), be related to any other modifications in the insect, perhaps of a physiological kind?
4. How is spotting inherited and what influence, if any, is exerted by environmental factors?

As in any research, questions which appeared initially to be clear-cut and discrete turned out to have wider ramifications and to merge one into another. In the account that follows it will be seen how widely differing lines of enquiry tended to converge while the same questions were often repeated in different contexts.

Selective agents and spotting

So far, one of the most significant findings in our studies of the meadow brown has been the extraordinary stability of spot-distribution in both sexes. Throughout the central part of the butterfly's range from Britain eastwards across Europe and into Asia Minor, the General European pattern apparently prevails in spite of extreme variations of climate, geology, and vegetation. It therefore seemed to us inconceivable that spotting was not, at least to some extent, under hereditary control. This being so, in investigating the nature of spot-stability and change, we were concerned with the mechanism of evolution. What were the selective agents responsible for bringing the process about?

In the early 1960s, the generally accepted view of spotting was that it had little or no relevance for the adult. Such evidence as was available suggested that pairing between individuals with different spot numbers was at random and that spots *per se* had no connection with any aspect of adult behaviour, such as courtship. However, it is well known that in genetic systems generally, single genes often exert multiple effects. Could it be, therefore, that the hereditary mechanism controlling spotting also influenced important features of an adaptive kind in other stages of the life cycle, such as the larva? Such a hypothesis seemed to us to be well worth testing. If it were possible to obtain meadow brown larvae as early in their development as possible and shield them from selective agents such as predators by rearing them in the laboratory, we would be able to compare the spot-distributions of the experimental insects with their counterparts flying in nature. Any differences between the two would presumably be due to the effects of selective influences some of which might become apparent during the period of captivity.

For an experiment of this kind it was necessary to find a population of meadow browns which,

(a) exhibited a typical spot-distribution in both males and females,
(b) was stable in respect of spotting, both inter- and intra-seasonally,
(c) was large enough to permit adequate sampling of larvae and adults.

The meadow brown at Middleton East

After much searching we eventually found a colony which conformed to these requirements inhabiting a small patch of chalk downland of some 7 hectares about 4 km east of Andover (Hampshire). The locality was known as Middleton East due to its proximity to the village of that name. It was surrounded on all sides by dense deciduous woodland which had apparently housed an ammunition dump during the last war. As observation soon showed, it provided an impenetrable barrier to the flight of meadow browns. From mark–release–recapture data we estimated the size of the colony to fluctuate annually between approximately 3000 and 10 000 insects.

Sampling the adult population over a period of five years (1956–60) showed its spot-distribution to be typical of southern England in both sexes, the males being unimodal at 2 spots and the females unimodal at 0.[38] During this time the female samples were homogeneous ($P = 0.2$). Unexpectedly, the males varied appreciably ($P < 0.01$) though not in response to any apparent ecological change. Our studies throughout the summer of 1960 established complete intra-seasonal homogeneity among both the females

$(P>0.3)$ and males $(P>0.3)$.[38] Evidently intra-seasonal shift (p. 70) was not a feature of the colony—a finding amply supported by our samples in subsequent years.

The next step was to obtain random collections of larvae. On consulting the relevant entomological literature we found a variety of conflicting information on the life cycle of the meadow brown, much of which turned out to be inaccurate. We therefore decided to approach the subject from the beginning using a combination of laboratory investigation and observation in the field. By now we had discovered how to induce the butterflies to pair and lay eggs in captivity when kept in square, muslin-covered cages with sides about 0.3 m long. The main requirements were warmth, light, and an abundant flow of air. The females tended to lay in the shade, so we attached strips of dark material to the outsides of the cages. This greatly facilitated the collection of eggs afterwards. Another requirement was a supply of liquid food. This was provided by means of 'synthetic flowers', consisting of plastic pot-scrubbers pressed down inside small plastic cups filled with dilute honey solution so that a butterfly could stand on the scrubber and insert its proboscis through the interstices of the scrubber into the liquid below. In this way newly emerged insects could be kept alive for a week or more.

Eggs laid in July or August hatch after about a fortnight and the tiny larvae immediately start feeding by day. By the onset of winter they have attained a length of a few millimetres. At this stage it is possible to collect them with a sweep net in daytime but it is a tedious operation as the caterpillars are difficult to see and easily damaged. Once cold weather begins, they hibernate but continue to feed spasmodically when conditions permit. Active feeding begins again in late April. By now the larvae have attained a length of about 10 mm and are a highly attractive food for insectivorous birds and small mammals. We discovered this to our cost by inadvertently keeping our laboratory stocks in an outhouse where they could be attacked by shrews. This no doubt explains why, at this stage of their development, meadow brown larvae are exclusively nocturnal feeders.

In order to obtain adequate samples and to save unnecessary travelling, it was desirable to be able to predict the weather conditions in which the larvae would be at their most active. This turned out to be much more difficult than we had imagined. The microclimate of the grass tufts where the animals live must bear little relation to the macroclimate above. Comparatively little attention appears to have been paid to the ecology of these communities, but it soon became clear that certain other species such as ants, slugs, and snails provided good indicators of larval activity. In general, we found that for successful collecting a minimum temperature of 10 °C was necessary, also a fairly heavy dew or light rain. The main food plants of the larvae at Middleton East proved to be a variety of grasses, particularly downy oat (*Helictotrichon pubescens*) and slender false-brome (*Brachypodium sylvaticum*).

Evolving a technique for collecting a random sample of caterpillars at night also posed problems, since the density of the population at Middleton was quite low. The procedure frequently advocated in the literature of picking the larvae by hand from the stems of grass using the light of a torch proved to be impracticable. The only reasonably efficient method of collecting was with a sweep net, but even with this the accumulation of an adequate sample was a laborious process, a catch of 40 larvae requiring a time expenditure of around 6 net-hours. We tried out two different types of net (Plate 18). The sledge net proved the more effective on smooth ground, but in the rough conditions of Middleton the sweep net was preferable. The area was studded with rabbit warrens which posed considerable hazards after dark. Our efforts to avoid them while wielding our nets caused great mirth among the local inhabitants. However, a reminder about the past history of the area and the possibility of unexploded bombs usually served to curb an excess of enthusiasm on their part.

Our preliminary efforts at sampling larval populations proved even less rewarding than we had expected, bearing in mind the density of adult butterflies at Middleton the previous summer. However, a chance observation in the laboratory threw unexpected light on our failure. We noticed that when feeding at night near the tips of the grass stems, the larvae were particularly sensitive to low-frequency vibrations. The slightest jolt of the bench on which their cages were standing caused them to curl up and drop to the floor of the cage where they remained motionless for ten minutes or more. Was our trampling over the area at Middleton East where we were subsequently to collect having a similar effect? To reduce

a

b

Plate 18   Types of net used for collecting meadow brown larvae: (a) heavy sledge net—good for level ground; (b) sweep net—better for rough ground. Note for both the position of the net in relation to the collector.

this possibility we were careful thereafter not to tread on the vegetation to be sampled and to ensure that collectors wielded their nets well clear of places where they themselves had walked (see Plate 18). The results of this revised technique were sensational!

Rearing larvae in captivity presented little difficulty and they thrived in the laboratory when kept in standard insect cages, feeding on the appropriate species of grass grown in pots. It soon became clear that larval mortality was due to two distinct causes, parasitization by the Hymenopteran ('Ichneumon') *Apanteles tetricus* and an unknown ailment subsequently identified as a bacterial infestation.[38] Typical examples of larval survival in the laboratory are provided by our results at Middleton East in 1959 and 1960, summarized in Table 23.

Table 23   Mortality among reared meadow brown larvae and pupae from Middleton East, 1959-60.

Year	Period of sampling	Total larvae	Mortality of larvae (per cent)	Percentage of mortality due to Apanteles	Mortality of pupae (per cent)
1959	9.v–31.v	48	10.4	– ⎫	
	1.vi–9.vii	220	31.8	78.6 ⎭	6.2
1960	26.iv–31.v	101	19.8	5.0 ⎫	
	1.vi–18.vii	259	39.3	73.5 ⎭	10.9

It will be noted that deaths were strongly seasonal. Those due to bacterial infection occurred predominantly among larvae collected early, while *Apanteles* accounted for the majority in those collected later. Mortality among pupae remained consistently at a fairly low level. This occurred invariably at the pigmented stage a few days prior to emergence and although not identified for certain, it seems likely that the pathogen concerned was bacterial.

Comparison of the reared adults with those flying at Middleton East revealed little difference in the males over the four years 1957-60 (*P* ranged from 0.95 to 0.10). In the females, however, there was a marked divergence among the reared insects emerging early which was clearly evident each year, their spot-values being far higher than those of their flying counterparts. A typical example is provided by the data for 1959 which are shown graphically in Fig. 28.

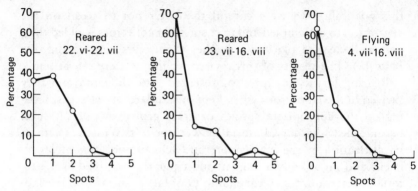

Figure 28   Spot distributions in reared and flying meadow brown females from Middleton East, 1959.

It will be noted from Table 23 that June to July was the period when infestation of larvae by *Apanteles* was at its highest. The reared butterflies which emerged in late July and August, and exhibited wild-type spotting, were thus derived from caterpillars which had managed to remain unaffected. Could it be that the level of spotting in the adult females was somehow related to the liability to parasitization of the larvae from which they were derived?

Random sampling of larvae

A basic assumption underlying our work at Middleton East was that sampling of larval populations was at random. If spotting in the adult was under genetic control, as it clearly must be to some extent, could the genes concerned possibly affect aspects of behaviour as well? For instance, in the larval stage, they might influence feeding behaviour determining whether a caterpillar tended to feed high up a grass stem or low down. Such a pattern could have accounted for the discrepancy between reared and flying females, since the former would presumably have been derived from larvae with a strong bias towards high feeding thus enhancing their likelihood of capture.

To test this hypothesis, swept larvae were observed in their breeding cages at night and divided according to their feeding behaviour into two groups—high feeding and low feeding. The division was obviously rather an artificial one, but as far as possible we maintained a degree of rigour by selecting certain arbitrary points on the grass stems to decide into which category each larva should be placed. The final selection was made as a result of examining the cages on four successive nights at a time when collecting at Middleton East would have taken place (between 2200 and 2300 hours). Perhaps surprisingly, the larvae seemed to exhibit under laboratory conditions a fairly consistent and characteristic pattern of feeding from night to night. Whether this represented in any way what happened in nature, it was of course impossible to say. A comparison of spot-distribution in the resulting adults showed that there was no significant difference in either sex between those derived from low- and high-feeding larvae. For the males $P > 0.30$, and in the females $P = 0.90$. As far as feeding behaviour was concerned, there thus seemed to be good reason for assuming that our samples of larvae were random.

The Cheesefoot Head population

Our findings at Middleton had shown a surprising level of consistency over a period of four years. Not only had we evolved a method for studying the effects of selective agents in larval populations, but it had also been possible to estimate the selection pressures operating against the later developmental stages in nature. Thus selective elimination of female meadow browns with 2 spots or more, emerging early at Middleton, was found to be of the order of 70 per cent. This provided an interesting comparison with the situation in the vicinity of the boundary area in East Cornwall where selection was the same order of magnitude, in the transition from a Southern English to an East Cornish spot-distribution (see Chapter 3).

But were the changes that we had observed at Middleton peculiar to that locality or of more widespread occurrence among meadow brown populations elsewhere? To answer this question it was obviously necessary to repeat the work in a different locality. Using the same criteria as we had applied in the selection of Middleton East, we found another suitable meadow brown population at Cheesefoot Head, near Winchester (Hampshire). Unlike the Middleton locality which was ungrazed by cattle, relatively flat, and isolated by woodland, Cheesefoot Head was heavily grazed, steeply sloping and part of a great expanse of agricultural land extending over many kilometres. As far as the butterflies were concerned, there was one other significant difference from Middleton in that the Cheesefoot Head population exhibited a strong tendency among the females towards intra-seasonal spot-variation. Sampling of larvae and rearing them in the laboratory revealed a situation comparable to that at Middleton.[39] The main cause of larval mortality was still *Apanteles tetricus* and a bacterial infection which, thanks to the help of Dr H. M. Darlow of the Microbiological Research Establishment, Porton, had been identified as being

Table 24 Samples of reared and flying meadow brown females from Cheesefoot Head, 1961.

Period	Date of emergence	Spots						Total	Spot average
		0	1	2	3	4	5		
Reared									
Early	12.vi–28.vi	17	28	21	7	1	–	74	1.28
Middle	29.vi–21.vii	33	33	22	3	–	–	91	0.95
Late	22.vii–23.viii	33	11	9	3	–	–	56	0.68
Flying									
Early	18.vi–29.vi	52	42	29	16	1	–	140	1.09
Middle	6.vii–15.vii	62	41	30	11	2	–	146	0.97
Late	19.viii–22.viii	103	44	17	2	–	–	166	0.51

associated with *Pseudomonas fluorescens*. Whether the bacterium was a primary pathogen or a secondary infection of a previously parasitized body remained open to speculation.

A comparison of the reared and flying adults in terms of spotting raised some interesting questions. As before, the males showed comparatively little variation. However, in the females which varied intra-seasonally, spot averages of the reared and flying populations on the wing at the same time conformed closely to one another[40] (see Table 24).

Comparison of the seasonal patterns of larval mortality and subsequent spotting of the adult female population revealed an interesting relationship between them. Insects emerging early (in June) had the highest spot-values (Table 24) and were derived from larvae whose mortality was attributable almost entirely to bacteria. Those appearing later with lower spotting were from larvae which had been subject to heavy elimination by *Apanteles*. Thus it seemed that bacteria tended to eliminate larvae destined to give rise to low spot-value adults while the ichneumon had the reverse effect.

Precisely what the causal relationship is, if any, between larval parasitization and adult female spotting has yet to be determined. Such additional evidence as exists at present is incomplete or largely circumstantial. Thus, when laboratory stocks of larvae reared from eggs laid by females of known pairings are decimated by bacteria to the extent of about 95 per cent (as those from southern England often are) the resulting adults are much more highly spotted than might have been expected. On the other hand, eight years' experience of collecting fourth and fifth instar larvae and rearing them in the laboratory, has enabled us to predict with some accuracy from the timing and intensity of *Apanteles* infestation what the spot-distribution of the emerging females was likely to be. In the populations we have studied, a high level of parasitization was invariably followed by low adult spotting and *vice versa*.

In theory, the testing of this hypothesis should not be difficult, but there are certain practical problems. During the late period of larval growth it is not difficult to acquire a large stock of *Apanteles* adults. In order to test their effects on adult female spotting, it is necessary to introduce them into cages containing first instar larvae derived from eggs of known parents. Attempts to do this have so far proved unsuccessful owing to the high subsequent mortality of the larvae due to bacterial infection. Such results as have been obtained are therefore unreliable. One of the chief problems of investigating the effects of bacteria on adult spotting is to control the level of infestation and hence the degree of larval mortality. To be successful, any experiment would necessitate the breeding of very large numbers of animals. Evidently, the meadow brown egg is sterile but the young larvae quickly become colonized by a complex bacterial population derived mainly from the surrounding vegetation. Being herbivores, some of these bacteria are essential in aiding the digestion of cellulose, and so the maintenance of caterpillars in a 'sterile' state is therefore impossible.

By contrast with the work at Middleton and Cheesefoot Head, Brakefield[19] has conducted similar experiments using larvae swept from populations at Buckley (Wales) and Cramond Island (Scotland). In neither was there a difference in spotting between the reared and flying adults of either sex. Perhaps significantly, although both samples of larvae were subject to a mortality of around 30 per cent, only a single death was due to a Braconid parasite, *Apanteles tetricus* or *A. tibialis*. Samples of larvae were also obtained from St Martin's, Isles of Scilly, and here again a comparison of reared and flying adults produced an unexpected result, the greatest divergence being among the males. The spot averages in the reared population were unusually high with values of 3, 4, and 5 spots in excess of expectation. Variation in the females also occurred but at a lower level, the tendency being, as at Middleton and Cheesefoot Head, towards increased spotting in the reared insects. Thus the balance of selective agents influencing the survival of different spot types evidently varies from one meadow brown population to another.

Ecological bacteriology of the meadow brown

If further progress was to be made in the elucidation of the role of bacteria as possible selective agents in the meadow brown, it was necessary to extend our studies of larval bacteriology. Accordingly, Professor Kennedy McWhirter and Dr Valerio Scali set about a comparative investigation of larvae from southern England, the Channel Islands, and the Scillies.[41] This involved plating out bacterial cultures from the various regions of the gut and the droppings (frass) of the caterpillars. As might be expected, there was considerable variation in the range of bacterial species present, both within populations and between them. However, some distinct patterns emerged. Thus, on grounds of adult spot-distribution, we might have expected larvae of English and Channel Island populations to be more alike than those of England and the Isles of Scilly. This seems to have been so, for Scillonian bacteria were found to respond positively to the Gram stain (Gram-postive) while those from English and Channel Island populations were mainly Gram-negative. Again, larvae obtained from two different Scillies habitats were found to contain distinct bacterial floras. This accords well with our experience of the adult butterflies in peripheral populations and at the extremity of their range; under the influence of minor ecological barriers they readily form discrete populations as evidenced by their differing spot-values.

When interpreting these results we must bear in mind that, so far, the only larvae tested have been those which have survived the severe process of selective elimination during the first three instars. A next step in the study of the ecological bacteriology of the meadow brown would be to extend the investigation to caterpillars in their early instars obtained from the field and reared under carefully controlled laboratory conditions. As yet, this has not been attempted.

Enzymes and adaptation

From its earliest days, our work on the meadow brown had suggested that spotting *per se* was unlikely to be of such adaptive significance to the adult that it could account for the remarkable instances of differential selection we had encountered in places like the boundary area in East Cornwall and the small islands of the Scillies. As we have seen, the investigations at Middleton East and Cheesefoot Head showed that the genetic system concerned with spot number does, indeed, control other characteristics as well, such as the susceptibility of the larva to parasitism. Since all adaptation depends ultimately on physiological processes there was clearly a need to identify some of these, or processes associated with them, and to investigate their variation in a manner comparable to the studies on spotting. Such thinking provided the background to the work of Dr Paul Handford at Oxford and others whose studies of the meadow brown were designed to determine whether populations characterized by particular spot-changes could also be seen to exhibit comparable patterns of enzyme variation.

The method of analysis used by Handford was acrylamide gel electrophoresis.[42] When an electric current is passed through a colloidal solution, any electrically charged particles present are attracted to the opposite pole. This property is made use of in the process of electrophoresis. If the particles suspended in the gel are enzymes (a form of protein) which are negatively charged, they are attracted to the positive pole. Different types of protein move at different rates, depending on their charge, so if a mixture is present

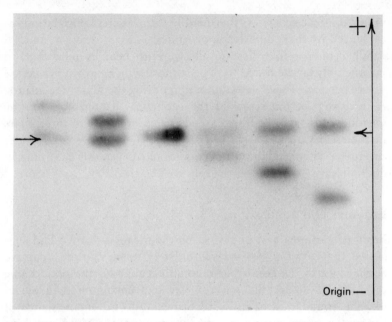

Plate 19   Starch-gel electrophoresis showing the six PGM variants found in the meadow brown. Horizontal arrows show the D band position. The six variants shown are, from the left, DF, DE, D, CD, BD, AD. Individual differences in the amount of enzyme are quite common (see the CD and D specimens).

a series of bands are formed, each corresponding to a different protein. After electrophoresis and appropriate staining, the resulting pattern of movement by the different enzyme variants along a column of gel is photographed. A typical result is shown in Plate 19. The transfer of insects caught in the West Country to the laboratory at Oxford necessitated their preservation in dry ice (solid carbon dioxide) in order to minimize deterioration. This presented some interesting administrative problems, not least gaining access to hotel deep freezers for use in a rather unorthodox role!

Handford succeeded in identifying two distinct enzyme systems in the meadow brown. One, with the slower mobility in electrophoresis, he designated Es-A1, Es-A2, and Es-An; that with the greater mobility was Es-Bo, Es-B1, and Es-B2. Evidently, there was no interaction between the two systems which existed independently of each other. Moreover, there appeared to be no genetic relationship between the esterase (enzyme) variants and variations in adult spotting. Enzmye analysis of male meadow browns showed them to be singularly invariable; in this they therefore resembled their hind-wing spotting. All had a trace of Es-A1, and where any gel banding could be detected in the Es-B region, this was was always in the B1 position.

Examination during 1969 and 1970 of some 25 localities in southern England ranging from east Dorset to west Cornwall, including the boundary area, revealed a general increase from east to west of insects with a single Es-A2 band. This trend was, however, reversed in the boundary area where the incidence of Es-A1 and Es-A2 underwent a marked change in frequency compared with the relatively stable condition elsewhere. In the Es-B system there was a significant increase of Es-B1 and a reduction of Es-B2 from east to west. However, in common with the A series, this also underwent interruption and reversal in the boundary area. These findings thus accorded closely with our data for spotting, notably in the change-over from Southern English to East Cornish stabilizations and the existence of the reverse cline effect in the vicinity of the boundary (see Chapter 3).

Handford also studied samples of meadow browns from nineteen localities in seven of the Isles of Scilly.[43] On the large islands of St Mary's and Tresco he found strong comparability in both the Es-A and Es-B systems, St Martin's occupying a somewhat intermediate position between them. Perhaps this was to be expected, bearing in mind the diversity of habitats on St Martin's and the fact that the evolution of discrete populations in ecologically isolated parts of the island was already known to have occurred (see Chapter 5). By contrast, the small islands studied proved each to be distinct, thereby conforming to the pattern already evident from their differing spot-distributions. Of particular interest was the light that Handford's work threw on the situations on White Island and Great Ganilly. It will be recalled that the gales during the winter of 1957 had virtually cut White Island into two, the respective populations of butterflies becoming markedly distinct from one another in their female spot-distributions. By 1970, following the gradual rejoining of the two parts of the island, the difference in spotting between the north and south ends had gradually become reduced and was now non-existent. Nonetheless, the Es-B system showed a clear distinction between the two ends ($P < 0.01$) while the Es-A values were similar ($P > 0.3$). Unfortunately, we have no evidence regarding the Es systems before or after separation. Indeed, the methods used by Handford for the analysis of esterases had not then been developed.

Comparable with White Island was the evidence provided by esterase distribution in the populations of the meadow brown on Great Ganilly. Having realized in 1956 that the northern and southern parts of the island supported distinct populations in terms of spot-distribution, we had thereafter sampled the two areas separately. The enzyme studies strongly confirmed the existence of a barrier. Thus, for the Es-B fraction, there was a clear-cut difference between north and south ($P < 0.02$), while for Es-A, a similar trend, although evident, just failed to attain the level of formal significance ($P < 0.10$).

A comparable approach to that of Dr Handford has been adopted by Dr Massimo Masetti and Dr Valerio Scali in their work on the meadow brown in Italy, much of which was described in Chapter 4. In an attempt to elucidate more clearly the genetic similarities and diversities existing among different populations, they used as a marker for electrophoretic analysis the enzyme phosphoglucomutase (PMG).[44] This plays an important part in carbohydrate metabolism, catalysing the conversion of glucose-1-phosphate to glucose-6-phosphate. Samples of butterflies were caught in the same localities as previously described (Fig. 19) and the second instar larvae used for electrophoresis were derived from eggs laid by post-aestivation females from Il Boschetto (see Chapter 4). A typical result of starch–gel electrophoresis is shown in Plate 19. Evidently, every animal possessed either one or two of six enzyme variants (A to F). An interesting deviation from Handford's findings with esterases was that for PGM no variation existed between the two sexes ($P > 0.9$). But, as with esterases, the distribution of PGM enzymes proved to be independent of spot-characteristics.

As explained earlier (Chapter 4), at the time of copulation a female receives from the male a large spermatophore which completely blocks her copulation pouch.[27] Evidence from the dissection of many female butterflies from different Italian sites and observation of mating behaviour, had reinforced beyond doubt the view that monogamy is the established breeding pattern. Electrophoresis therefore provides a means of following the transmission of PGM characteristics from mothers to their offspring. The results of such an experiment involving six females mated to unknown males are summarized in Table 25.

Table 25   Distribution of PGM in the offspring of six female meadow browns from Il Boschetto, 1975.

Family number	Maternal enzymes	Enzymes of offspring				
		BD	C	CD	D	Total
1034	D	–	–	–	1	1
1035	D	–	–	–	16	16
1080	CD	1	–	1	2	4
1090	CD	–	2	2	–	4
1091	CD	–	–	7	1	8
1092	D	–	–	–	2	2

From these results it is possible to predict with certainty the paternal enzymes in family 1080 which must have been BD, while in family 1035 it was probably DD; in family 1090, CC; and in family 1091, CD. Masetti and Scali found that the distribution of enzyme variants in different populations exhibited a characteristic pattern. Thus A and B were most frequent on the Italian mainland, while F was rare on the plains but relatively common on the neighbouring islands of Giglio and Elba (see Fig. 19).

The reliability of PGM determinations in both larvae and adults has enabled comparisons to be made between them and hence has provided a means of assessing differential survival in particular populations and the action of natural selection. As we have seen, actively feeding fourth and fifth instar larvae climb the grass blades at night and can then be collected by sweeping with a stout net (Plate 18). Masetti and Scali compared the PGM variants of the larvae with those of the subsequent adults. Their analysis revealed that selection, occurring between the late larval stages and imagines, was very strong,[45] in close parallel to the findings in relation to spot-distribution at Middleton and Winchester.[38, 39, 40] Evidently, the pupal stage must be a critical one for selection. Whether the selective agents concerned, whatever these may be, are acting directly on the PGM system it is hard to say. As Masetti and Scali have suggested, one explanation is that characteristics are being selected of an adaptively different kind, specifically linked to the gene system controlling PGM.

The work on PGM is particularly significant for two reasons. Not only has it added to our knowledge of the Mendelian mode of inheritance and the selection of enzyme variants, but it has also enabled a comparison to be made between enzyme distribution and spotting. Here, the degree of correspondence is striking. It is indeed remarkable that such different characters as pigment pattern on an insect's wings and its possession of certain enzyme variants of PGM, features with no apparent causal relationship, should nonetheless lead to the same conclusions regarding the pattern of stabilization in different populations. The picture of variation emerging from the study of PGM has clearly reinforced our assumption that spotting is under genetic control. As Masetti and Scali have pointed out,[44] the results are also in line with the findings of Handford concerning the distribution of esterase systems in the boundary area of south-west England[42] and in the Isles of Scilly.[43] But whereas in the esterases a marked difference between males and females seemed to occur, for PGM both sexes showed the same kind and degree of variation.

As a result of their work with PGM, Masetti and Scali have concluded that, throughout their range, meadow brown populations can be divided roughly into two groups.[46] The eastern group, typified by the Italian mainland, exhibits frequencies of PGM D (about 55 per cent), C (about 30 per cent), and B (about 5 per cent). The comparable figures for the western group which includes Roumania, Sardinia, Spain, and Britain, are D (>70 per cent), C (about 15 per cent), and F or E (about 8 per cent). Support for the validity of this division is provided by the fact that it accords closely with that postulated by Thomson[6] (see Chapter 1) on the grounds of genital structure. Such data as are available for southern England[46] suggest an increase in most PGM values from east to west (Eggardon and Rowden Moor) with a marked discontinuity between the mainland and the Isles of Scilly (St Martin's). Unfortunately, no information is at present available for the boundary area.

Another important aspect of PGM has been the stability of its variants which have remained remarkably constant in their occurrence from one locality to another. Where differences have occurred, they have done so in an orderly manner which could frequently be related to changing ecological conditions. They have thus paralleled closely the comparable situation in spotting.

The inheritance of spotting

Our widespread studies of the meadow brown have provided abundant indications that spot-distribution must be under some form of hereditary control. Indeed, the remarkable stabilizations existing in southern Britain and across Europe would be inexplicable were this not so. However, such evidence was only circumstantial and there was obviously an urgent need for more direct information. In setting up a breeding programme two obstacles had to be overcome. As we have seen, a major cause of larval mortality in populations such as those near Winchester was bacterial infection.[39] Moreover, there was some evidence that the death rate was differential in relation to spotting, tending to eliminate larvae destined to become low spot-value adults. For effective breeding it was therefore necessary to find a population of butterflies where bacterial infestation was at a minimum. McWhirter and Scali fortunately succeeded in identifying such a population in the Isles of Scilly where, as previously noted, larvae from different localities often vary greatly in their bacterial microfloras.[41] In general, such larvae thrived in captivity provided they were kept under conditions of fairly constant temperature.[47]

A second problem concerned the mode of inheritance of spotting and the likelihood that spot numbers depended upon the additive effects of a series of genes (multifactorial). But whereas in a typical situation such as human height, grades of variation conform to a characteristic normal distribution represented by a bell-shaped curve, in the meadow brown they take the form of a series of quantal steps moving from one spot-value to the next. Assessing the hereditary component of spotting is comparable to the problem facing commercial breeders of plants and animals, who wish to know what proportion of the variation they observe in their stocks is attributable to environmental effects such as feeding, and is therefore not inherited, and how much to the influence of genes, and therefore inherited. Suppose the variance* of a particular characteristic due to genes with additive effects is V_G and the total variance of the population including that due to environmental factors is V_T, then $V_G/V_T =$ the *heritability* of that characteristic. Heritability is an important parameter both academically and commercially, for it enables a prediction to be made regarding the outcome of selecting for a particular characteristic such as milk yield in cows or egg weight in poultry.

Applying this principle to the meadow brown, McWhirter raised broods of butterflies from known pairings using a strain from the Isles of Scilly that was largely immune to the effects of bacteria in the larval stage.[47] At 15 °C heritability of males proved to be low at 0.14, while at 22 °C it was 0.47 ± 0.20, indicating a fairly strong environmental component of variance (for total genetic control and no environmental influence, the figure for heritability would be 1). By contrast, the comparable figures for females at 15 °C were 0.63 ± 0.14 (or 0.83, depending on the method of calculation used and the extent to which the small size of the broods was taken into account), and at 22 °C, 0.78 ± 0.16.

Brakefield[19] has also obtained limited information from broods obtained in the area of Liverpool and from St Martin's, Isles of Scilly, all of which were subject to mortality exceeding 95 per cent. He calculated that heritability of spot numbers in males was 0.78 ± 0.91 and in females 0.49 ± 0.98.

Although at present somewhat limited, the results of breeding the meadow brown under laboratory conditions have confirmed our assumptions, made on other grounds, that spotting in the meadow brown is an inherited characteristic. As Ford has pointed out,[22] it is not uncommon for the genetic control of variation to differ in the two sexes. Indeed, instances are known, as in the white females (variety *helice*) of the clouded yellow butterfly (*Colias croceus*), where the effect of a gene influencing pigmentation is inhibited altogether and fails to express itself in the male.

---

* Variance is a measure of variation. Where the variations in a population are expressed as deviations from the population mean, the variance is the mean of the squared deviations.

Adult behaviour and spot-variation

From our early studies of meadow brown populations in England and the Isles of Scilly we concluded that hind-wing spotting was of little or no significance for the adults of either sex. The limited information we accumulated, much of it incidental, suggested that mating in nature between different spot types was at random and that the pattern and extent of adult movement were also unrelated to spotting. The work of Dr Paul Brakefield[19, 48] has demonstrated admirably how systematic observation and a quantitative approach can reveal important issues which are liable to be overlooked in a more superficial and casual treatment. The meadow brown population studied by Brakefield in 1976-8 was at Hightown, near the coast to the north of Liverpool. It proved well suited for an ecological study for a number of reasons. The locality was a homogeneous piece of grassland occupying an area of approximately 188 m × 75 m (1.4 ha). It has remained undisturbed by the inroads of agriculture for at least twenty years and this had permitted the build-up of an established butterfly population. The distribution of adults tended to be somewhat clumped (particularly in the males), some areas apparently being more favoured than others. The larvae, too, were localized in their distribution. The density of adults for the two sexes combined was about two per 12.5 m² in 1976, but in subsequent years was much reduced. The spot average in both sexes was relatively high, which had the advantage of ensuring the presence of an adequate proportion of the higher spotted types, particularly among the females. The population was visited continuously during three successive summers for periods of twelve consecutive days (1976) or longer (1977 and '78). Each capture was marked so as to permit individual identification and scored for spotting before being released as close as possible to the point where it had been caught. This necessitated the establishment of a precise recording system based on a grid of 7.5 m squares.

During the period of study, mark–release–recapture estimates in 1976 suggested a maximum daily population size of about 450 females and 350 males. Calculation of daily survival rates showed no significant differences or trends among the various spot types or between the sexes. Of particular interest was Brakefield's study of behaviour patterns relating to movement. Among females there was a clear indication of increasing dispersal, measured by the mean minimum distances travelled ('move lengths'—ML), with increasing spot numbers in all three years. There was also evidence that for a particular spot number, females showing a bias towards costality (see p. 74) tended to exhibit a lower dispersal rate than the others. Thus in 1976, 0 ($\simeq$ 30 m), costal 1 ($\simeq$ 28 m) and costal 2 ($\simeq$ 38 m) individuals all showed a ML of 28–38 m. By contrast, splay 2 females had a ML of 57.5 m, while the other more highly spotted individuals also showed a relative increase in ML. A similar trend towards greater dispersal with increasing spot number seemed to be evident in the males in 1976 and 1977 but this was not found in 1978. From existing evidence, the conclusion therefore seems to be that dispersal distances in the two sexes are about the same but the males fly more often and are generally the more active. Moreover, because of their searching behaviour in suitable areas, males are more likely to remain close to the starting point, while females tend to fly away from the place of release. Brakefield also tested the hypothesis that capture in a net (which could be construed as simulating an attack by a potential predator) modified the pattern of subsequent behaviour on release. Although an attractive idea, it did not prove to be supported by the experimental evidence for either sex.

The work at Hightown also served to reinforce the point made earlier (Chapter 1), that for much of the flight period the distributional pattern of meadow brown colonies suggests that the two sexes are largely distinct populations. Thus Brakefield observes that whereas the females were often caught while they were feeding on flowers, the males tended to be encountered round the perimeter of the population along tracks and in areas of intermediate height, grassy vegetation. Such a distribution correlates closely with the differing resource requirements of the two sexes. While the females need sources of nectar (essential for the maturation of eggs) and sites for oviposition, the primary objective of males is to locate and mate with previously unmated females. This they achieve usually when the females are at rest or feeding. The strategy adopted seems to be first to locate a suitable area—one containing a high density of unmated females which can be identified and approached; then to cover and explore it as intensively as possible.

Evidence provided by beak marks on butterflies' wings suggests that birds are frequent predators on meadow browns of both sexes. Brakefield suggests that marginal spot patterning of the wings, when it is present, could serve an important function in deflecting a predator's attention away from the body of the insect. Thus males tend to exhibit a well developed and more or less uniform pattern of spotting on the hind-wings, the eye spot on the fore-wings being considerably smaller than in the female. For an active insect such spotting would have a generalized deflective role. In the females, emphasis is on the development of the fore-wing spots which are usually single, much larger than in the males, and frequently bipupilled, those on the hind-wings being reduced and often absent. Here we have a situation which is widespread in the animal kingdom: a structure which can be flashed in time of danger as a means of confusing a potential predator and deflecting attack from a vital part of the body. When a female is resting with the wings folded the spots are hidden from view; they are usually only revealed when she is alarmed or about to fly. Thus, as a generalization, it could be that selection for higher and larger hind-wing spotting is characteristic of those butterflies that tend to be most active. The less active the individuals, the less will hind-wing spot-development occur. Supporting this hypothesis is the difference in activity between the two sexes and the finding that in the female there is a marked trend among more spotted individuals to exhibit higher dispersal rates, while in males a similar trend is much less apparent. Males, as we have already seen in previous chapters, show a narrower range of spot pattern variation both on the fore- and hind-wings. Moreover, their populations tend to be more stable in spot-frequency than those of females. As Brakefield points out, this suggests that selection may have had a stabilizing effect in the males but a relatively disruptive one in the females.

Reasoning along these lines could help to explain why variation in spot patterns occurs and the role of visual selection in controlling it. Indeed, we can see why spots are present at all and why marked differences occur between the sexes and within them. Clearly, there is a need to study in much greater detail the microenvironmental conditions that butterflies of different sex and spot type tend to encounter and select, also details of their wing movements and positioning in varying situations. As was pointed out earlier in this chapter, we also need much more complete genetic data on the mode of inheritance of spotting. These are fields where the researcher and the amateur naturalist with a capacity for careful observation and meticulous recording, both have important contributions to make.

7

卷卷卷卷卷卷卷卷卷卷卷卷卷卷卷卷卷卷卷卷卷卷卷卷

Conclusions and implications

A feature of all knowledge is that it tends to increase exponentially; that is to say, it accumulates in a manner similar to compound interest. From the answer to one question a new set of questions arises, and these in turn provoke further questioning. As understanding increases in depth, so the breadth of enquiry expands also, radiating out fanwise. Thus, in order to keep the span of a piece of research within manageable bounds, it is frequently necessary to decide the point at which its coverage should be curtailed. Such decisions are often somewhat arbitrary and therefore difficult to make.

In the previous chapters, one of my aims has been to show how a piece of ecological research proceeded and the kinds of decisions that had to be taken at different stages. During the work we were frequently engaged in prolonged discussions regarding the most appropriate course to take at a particular juncture. Should we concentrate on the northern or the southern transect; or both together? Ought we to pay more attention to peripheral areas such as the Isles of Scilly or Scotland, or to the continent of Europe? Was there a need to place more emphasis on the experimental side of the work? The answers to such questions depended on a number of factors whose relative significance varied with circumstances—personal (the availability of the necessary manpower); economic (the provision of adequate resources, particularly finance and time); intellectual (the significance of a particular line of enquiry in relation to the whole and the extent of our relevant background knowledge). Regarding the latter, advances in our understanding and the development of new experimental techniques in such fields as cytology (e.g. high power microscopy) and physiology (e.g. electrophoresis) have stimulated investigations in areas like differential sexual selection of larvae and the adaptive significance of enzyme systems (see Chapter 6) which would not have been contemplated twenty years ago.

Our studies of ecological genetics in the meadow brown butterfly spanning a period of more than forty years must rank as one of the longest continuous investigations ever conducted on a species of animal or plant. In the remaining pages, an attempt will be made to assess our main achievements so far and to indicate areas of research related to them from which profitable lines of enquiry might be developed in future.

Quite early in our sampling of meadow brown populations on the British mainland and elsewhere, it became clear that, judged by a number of parameters such as spot-distribution, spot-placing, spot average and enzyme distribution, the species presented a picture of extraordinary stability. More detailed investigations of spotting were to reveal the existence of a Southern English stabilization extending westwards from the east coast to the vicinity of east Cornwall. Later it transpired that, far from being a phenomenon peculiar to Britain, the stabilization was much more extensive and included the whole of central Europe and part of Asia Minor (General European distribution). Its existence is the more remarkable when we remember the diversity of ecological conditions involved including profound changes in the physical environment like temperature, rainfall and soil composition. True, extreme environmental fluctuations such as the drought which occurred in the Isles of Scilly in 1957 (see Chapter 5) can be related to temporary upsets in the stabilized patterns of variation (second order variations) but, as our researches have shown, the first order patterns are usually re-established quite quickly once ecological conditions return to normal. We still have much to learn about the conditions that prevail in the microhabitats of plants and animals. Our extensive sampling of larval populations has served to highlight the fact that the microclimatic environment of a grass tuft is very different from the macroclimate a few feet above. There is an area here for much further investigation. Among other things, this could add to our knowledge of the characteristic behaviour patterns of such animals as the larvae of Lepidoptera, an understanding of which is essential for anyone attempting to obtain random samples of their populations. Such information as we obtained was acquired entirely empirically as a result of success and failure.

One of the advantages of working in the south of England has been that it has proved relatively easy to study the meadow brown at the extremity of its westerly range. On theoretical grounds we might expect that in such circumstances a species could find itself less well adapted to its environment than elsewhere and so exhibit a tendency towards an increase in variation. Such sensitivity has proved to be an outstanding feature of meadow brown populations in the west. Thus, in the Isles of Scilly, the Southern English spot-stabilization breaks down and each of the small islands studied exhibits its own peculiar spot-distribution. Detailed information on populations in other parts of the animal's range is scarce, but such evidence as exists, for instance from the Tuscan islands, suggests strongly that the same situation may obtain. Moreover, it may well be that variants such as spotting and enzyme distribution are not only indicators of local stabilizations but also serve to complement other parameters such as the varying anatomy of the reproductive apparatus, in establishing the transition from one species to another, for instance from *Maniola jurtina* in Europe to *M. telmessia* in Western Asia (Chapter 4). Further study of meadow brown populations in such areas as the Iberian Peninsula could be a valuable adjunct to our work in the south-west of Britain.

The boundary phenomenon (Chapter 3) representing a more or less abrupt discontinuity between one stabilization and another, has now been established as a feature of meadow brown populations both in the West Country and elsewhere. In attempting to analyse such a situation, a major problem is to establish the circumstances in which one form of population changes into another in the absence of a recognizable ecological barrier (sympatry) and with an appreciable amount of gene-flow going on between populations. We are still far from understanding the nature of the selective agents that control the distribution of such variants as spotting. However, for sympatry to be achieved, a prime requirement is that powerful forces determining differential survival should be in operation. We now know that such forces are widespread among populations of plants and animals. The situation in the boundary area of the meadow brown provides an admirable illustration, where we have estimated the selective elimination of certain spot-classes to be of the order of 65 per cent or more.[22] In such circumstances and using sufficiently sensitive parameters, we might expect microevolutionary changes in populations to be detectable in a relatively short period of time. Our studies of the meadow brown on Tean, Isles of Scilly, have shown this supposition to be true. In response to ecological conditions which became drastically altered as a result of the cessation of grazing by cattle, a significant change in spot-distribution among the populations to the north-west of the island was detected in the course of only two generations (Chapter 5). That such findings are by no means unique is illustrated by recent researches on many other species, the well known work of Kettlewell on the typical speckled and black (melanic) forms of the peppered moth, *Biston betularia*, and the relationship of their distribution to different degrees of industrial pollution,[22] providing an outstanding example.

The degree of consistency from year to year presented by the various spot-stabilizations in the meadow brown strongly suggests that the capacity to develop a range of spot patterns is inherited to some extent. If it were not, we would expect to find a situation in which the degree of variation in different populations fluctuated from one year to the next in accordance with changing environmental conditions. However, such evidence for spot-heritability is only circumstantial. Direct evidence for the inheritance of spotting, although now available (as explained in Chapter 6), has proved more difficult to obtain than we originally supposed. The reason for this is that certain bacteria exert a selective effect on larvae (for instance through their susceptibility to the disease 'black death') which is evidently also related to adult spot numbers, although the nature of the relationship is still unknown. Incidentally, it now seems doubtful whether larval parasitization by the 'ichneumon', *Apanteles tetricus*, also plays a part in influencing the spotting of adults, as was at one time believed. In our early work, selective influences that might have operated in the adult such as differential pairing relative to spot numbers or selection by predators such as birds were largely discounted. However, recent work by Brakefield[48] has thrown new light on the subject, suggesting that the behaviour of adult butterflies carrying different spot patterns differs appreciably in both sexes, for instance in the extent of their movement. This is another area in which further study would be profitable and is badly needed.

Evidence that a gene system may have multiple effects, such as governing behavioural activity in the adult and controlling susceptibility of the larva to bacterial infection, is now widespread. A typical example is provided by the peppered moth, *Biston betularia* (see above). Kettlewell[49] has shown that, in some larval populations inhabiting polluted industrial areas, larvae destined to give rise to the typical form of adults tend to feed rapidly and pupate relatively early. Those due to develop into melanic (*carbonaria*) moths feed more slowly and pupate a month or more later. Typical larvae are known to react adversely to polluted vegetation and to suffer a high mortality from eating it. Kettlewell suggests that selection for rapid growth may favour the typical form by enabling it to avoid the worst effects of pollution which gradually accumulate throughout the summer. The larvae of *carbonaria* are evidently well adapted to eating polluted food. However, slow feeding may have the additional advantage of enabling the caterpillars to rid themselves of toxic materials which could otherwise accumulate in their bodies. Thus the gene system which confers advantage and disadvantage in the adult also effects survival in the larval stage as well.

The most powerful ecological influence on Earth is man. Indeed, it is doubtful if any ecosystems now exist that are not influenced directly or indirectly by human activities. A classic example of this has already been mentioned, namely industrial melanism[22]—the tendency for a range insect species such as moths and ladybirds to evolve dark forms in areas subject to pollution due to the development of the pigment melanin in their wings and bodies. As far as the meadow brown is concerned, the effects of pollution appear to have had little effect on the numbers of established populations and the distribution of variants such as spotting. Nor is there much evidence that the widespread use of herbicides to control weeds on agricultural land and road verges has caused an appreciable decline in numbers. By far the greatest challenge of recent years to the survival of the butterfly has resulted from drastic changes in agricultural practice. As explained earlier, the insect is a colonist of grassland, the caterpillar feeding on a wide variety of grass species.

Twenty years ago, land used for the grazing of cattle tended to remain unploughed for many years, thus enabling large populations of the butterfly to build up together with a supply of broad-leaved flowering plants such as knapweed, *Centaurea nigra*, to which the adult insects are attracted as a source of water and food. But with the advent of high-intensity farming, a ley may well be ploughed and reseeded as often as once every four years. No sooner have the butterfly populations started to become established than their habitat is destroyed. Such practice has had a profound effect on the local distribution of the species which now tends to be confined to marginal land round the edges of fields, to roadside verges (the motorways are particularly important in this respect) and to the few 'old' areas of grassland still remaining.

In relation to human interference, the phenomenon of industrial melanism and the situation facing grass-feeding species of butterflies such as the meadow brown provide an interesting contrast. In areas of the midlands and north polluted by industry, insects possessing melanic forms which had previously occurred as a rarity, were faced with conditions in which melanism was at a selective advantage due to the concealment afforded from predatory birds and certain physiological advantages such as the tolerance by the larva of polluted food (mentioned above). As a result, there was a tendency for melanic forms to replace the typical ones, establishing new numerical equilibria between them, depending on such factors as the degree of pollution and the intensity of selection. In the meadow brown (particularly in southern England where most of our work has been carried out) the nature of the animal's environment has not changed appreciably; only its extent. We would therefore expect that in spite of changes in agricultural practice and a drastic reduction in the requisite ecological conditions, the form of the meadow brown would have remained unaltered. This is precisely what our studies of spot-distribution in the butterfly have shown.

Some topics for further study

If this book has succeeded in stimulating the reader to think about problems of adaptive change in plant and animal populations and to consider the possibility of pursuing some aspect of the subject further, it will have achieved its purpose. Of recent years there has been a spate of books covering various aspects of ecology and natural history, particularly systematics (identification). There has also been a great increase in field studies of all kinds among amateur naturalists, students, and at a more professional level. Yet it is a sad fact that many of these activities (perhaps the majority) proceed little further than the recording stage; the making of species lists and descriptions of their habitats. Many of our studies of the meadow brown recorded here were carried out in our spare time. For instance, all the experimental work at Middleton (Chapter 6) belongs to this category. Much of the time during the early days of our research was spent in evolving new techniques such as methods of marking butterflies and estimating the size of populations. Today, many of the basic experimental requirements for this kind of work are well established so the modern researcher is, as it were, off to a flying start. With a view to stimulating further studies in this field, the remainder of the chapter is concerned with enquiries which could prove profitable, no matter at what level of sophistication they were conducted. The theme throughout is variation, and the populations involved are all those of butterflies.

As our work on the meadow brown has shown, variation in an animal or plant is always potentially interesting, although at the outset of a study it is seldom clear how much of observed variation is due to environmental effects and how much is inherited. Butterflies, being relatively large, often plentiful, easy to catch, and sometimes highly variable, can provide admirable material for this sort of investigation.

(a) VARIATION IN SIZE

Several butterfly species are known to exhibit considerable variations in size. Thomson[50] has drawn attention to a number of variants in the meadow brown including wingspan. The race occurring in the Isle of Man appears to be the smallest known in Britain with an average wingspan of 45.2 mm. This compares with an average for the rest of Britain of 48.0 mm and for Ireland of 51.9 mm. Thomson records one male from the Manx race with a wingspan of only 36 mm and it could well be that other such races occur in localized and isolated habitats which have evolved on their own and have so far been overlooked.

Other species which have developed dwarf forms include the grayling, *Hipparchia semele*, which has evolved a race on Great Orme's Head, North Wales, with an average wing-expanse of about 41 mm in the male and 43 mm in the female, comparable measurements of the normal form being 48 mm and 52 mm respectively. Similarly, the silver-studded blue, *Plebejus argus*, has developed a dwarf form in the same area, the males averaging about 25.5 mm and the females 21.5 mm; each about 4 mm less than usual. Professor Ford[3] has described dwarf specimens of the orange-tip, *Anthocharis cardamines*, and similar size variants have been recorded in a number of other species as well. Sometimes the environmental conditions in which dwarfs occur suggest a possible reason for their evolution, as in the somewhat extreme conditions prevailing on Great Orme's Head. In other species, such as the orange-tip, size variations, although widely reported, do not seem to be related to any particular set of conditions. Incidentally, it is of interest that in species where dwarfs occur, these tend to grow more rapidly and emerge earlier than the normal form, suggesting that the gene system controlling adult size influences the rate of growth as well; the relationship between speed of development and the attainment of maturity.

(b) VARIATION IN PATTERN AND COLOUR
Mention was made in Chapter 1 of a wide range of spotting in such diverse species as the hedge brown, *Pyronia tithonus*, and the common blue, *Polyommatus icarus*, which provide opportunities for further investigation along similar lines to our work on the meadow brown. Some variable species possess more complex patterns and an example was given in Chapter 2 of one way in which prolonged and careful study of the marsh fritillary, *Euphydryas aurinia*, led not only to a better understanding of the butterfly itself but also to a fundamental advance in biological thinking. Our own preliminary studies of variation in the common blue, *Polyommatus icarus* (Chapter 2), provide another instance of findings which could well be taken further. As in the meadow brown, spot pattern is evidently a sensitive parameter for gauging environmental adjustment and increasing instability as the insect nears the extremity of its distribution.

Unlike the meadow brown, where variations in spot-distribution tend to take place in quantal steps from one stabilized pattern to another, some species exhibit a gradient of variation (cline) from one value to the next throughout all or part of their geographical range. A typical example is provided by the large heath, *Coenonympha tullia*, which exhibits a number of sub-species whose distribution is connected by transitional forms. Thus in the Hebrides the colour of the insect is pale brown above and greyish on the hind-wings beneath with virtually no eyespots. Further south, in Cumberland, the colour is a darker brown with well developed eyespots in both sexes, while in Staffordshire and Shropshire, the southern extremity of its range, the species shows maximum darkening in colour and in the development of eyespots. Here again, little is known of the circumstances in which transitional forms occur and these would repay further study.

(c) VARIATION IN BEHAVIOUR

As the recent work of Dr Brakefield, described in Chapter 6, has clearly shown,[48] the study of behaviour in butterflies such as their patterns of movement can be of great importance in helping to elucidate the significance of other variants such as spot-distribution. This is an aspect of the subject which has, as yet, scarcely been explored and could yield interesting and worthwhile results. Apart from the meadow brown where plenty still remains to be done, variable species such as the hedge brown, *Pyronia tithonus*, would seem to be particularly suitable subjects for investigation.

A striking feature of some butterfly species is that, in spite of being agile fliers, their range of movement is nonetheless surprisingly small. Migrants such as the clouded yellow (*Colias croceus*), having travelled great distances, will then settle down in a small locality and remain there for the rest of their lives. As an exercise with students some years ago, we laid out a grid consisting of a number of 50 m squares marked with string in the middle of a large colony of the common blue, *Polyommatus icarus*, near Winchester. We captured as many butterflies as we could, marked them (a colour dot from a felt pen on a hind-wing) and liberated them again in their respective squares, each being given a specific area mark. The colony was visited daily over a ten-day period and the distribution of the butterflies recorded, any unmarked individuals being captured, marked and released in the square where they were found. In general, the insects tended to remain in their respective squares and where greater movement occurred, it was nearly always no more than from one square to the next. The most powerful factor upsetting the distribution was a strong wind, but once this had subsided a new stable pattern returned.

Some colour variants are quite distinct from one another and may even occur in one sex only. This is likely when the dimorphism involves a considerable difference in appearance, owing to the visual stimulus to copulation exercised by the male, as in the two forms of the female clouded yellow, *Colias croceus*; the orange *croceus* form and the pale variety *helice*. It has long been known that the two varieties are inherited but their significance, if any, has never been demonstrated conclusively. A comparable situation occurs in a number of other *Colias* species such as the North American clouded yellow, *Colias eurytheme*, and here it has been shown that while the pale form is the rarer at low altitudes, at higher elevations and in cooler conditions its incidence increases. In a mixed population, if the time at which specimens are caught is recorded, the frequency of the white phase is found to be highest in the early morning and lower towards noon; it may or may not rise again in the afternoon.

Some years ago Professor Ford and I had the opportunity of testing the hypothesis that the situation in *Colias eurytheme* also applied to the two forms of *Colias croceus*. In the summer of 1947 the species was unusually abundant and this gave us an opportunity to make counts of the incidence of the orange and pale forms of the female in a large clover field (the food of the larva) in Cornwall.[51] Our results are summarized in Table 26 below.

Combining the results of the morning and evening captures, 36.4 ± 7.3 per cent of the females were of the pale form, while in

Table 26　Incidence of orange and pale forms of the female clouded yellow, *Colias croceus*, in a clover field, 1947.

Time	Orange females	Pale females	Total
Up to 11.00	21	13	34
After 17.30	7	3	10
Early and late combined	28	16	44
Noon to 15.30	20	4	24

the middle of the day the percentage was 16.6 ± 7.5. The difference is 19.8 ± 10.5 and since it is less than twice its standard error ($2 \times 10.5 = 21$) it cannot be regarded as significant. However, the result is strongly suggestive that the situation in *Colias eurytheme* may well be true of *C. croceus* as well, although larger numbers would be needed to establish it with certainty.

The clouded yellow is unfortunately only a migrant to Britain and therefore the opportunities for repeating this work are rather remote. However, it should not be a difficult matter on the continent of Europe since the species is indigenous in countries such as France and Germany, where it frequents agricultural fields planted with sainfoin, *Onobrychis viciifolia*, and lucerne, *Medicago sativa*. A valuable aspect of this sort of study is that it illustrates a way of investigating the possibility that structural and other variations may be related to behaviour. It could therefore be widely applicable to other species of British butterflies.

(d) VARIATION IN PUPAE AND LARVAE
In a number of butterfly species the pupae are subject to considerable variation but this has been studied only incompletely. As we noted in Chapter 1, the pupae of the meadow brown vary somewhat in the depth of green colouration and degree of black striping, but these differences do not seem to be related to characteristics in the adult such as spot-distribution. There is evidence that the colours of some pupae may be related to the environmental conditions in which they are formed. Thus, those of the small white, *Pieris rapae*, are green or brown depending on their background (cryptic), while those of the distasteful large white, *P. brassicae*, make themselves more conspicuous (aposematic). Again, the pupa of the small tortoiseshell, *Aglais urticae*, is yellowish brown when attached to the food plant (nettle) but grey-black when on a fence or tree trunk. Numerous experiments have been performed to test selection by predators such as birds of pupae occurring naturally and placed artificially in different positions and against varying backgrounds. For reference to these the reader should consult the appropriate literature.[3]

When rearing populations of meadow brown larvae (see Chapter 6), we noted that individuals seemed to exhibit fairly consistent behaviour in electing to feed high up or low down the grass stems.

Although we never investigated this, it may be that the same kind of preference applied to sites for pupation. It is certainly a fact that in our breeding cages, some pupae were found adhering to the grass stems at varying levels while others were found on the floor. There could be interesting differences in behaviour here which would repay further study. Larvae, too, are subject to considerable diversity but little is known for certain about the factors which cause it. On the whole they are far less variable than the imagines. As Brakefield has pointed out,[48] a good example is the hedge brown, *Pyronia tithonus*, where last instar larvae show marked environmental variation, being either bright green or a shade of brown. The proportion of each colour appears to be affected by the density of the population prior to their last moult, while physical factors such as light, temperature, and humidity may also exert an effect. Unfortunately, little is known about the density of larval populations in the field so at present it is not possible to evaluate the relative contribution of biotic and physical factors to the occurrence of colour differences under natural conditions.

Another aspect of larval variation deserving further study is the relatively common situation where a species has more than one food plant. The plants in question may well require different ecological conditions and hence will give rise to butterfly populations that are effectively isolated from one another. Are any differences detectable between such larval populations? A typical example is the green-veined white, *Pieris napi*, whose natural food plants include the cuckoo flower, *Cardamine pratensis*, and garlic mustard, *Alliaria petiolata*. In captivity the caterpillar is also known to eat garden 'nasturtium' *Tropaeolum* sp. Dr Willcox and I studied the feeding behaviour of the green-veined white in the Winchester area,[52] where the cuckoo flower occurs in damp fenland and garlic mustard in the shaded areas of woods and high hedges. The two kinds of locality were widely separated and, although we did not carry out marking experiments on the adult butterflies, there seems little doubt that the populations were isolated from one another. Our original intention had been to collect eggs from wild females laid on the three different food plants but limitations of time and availability of adult *napi* made this impossible. We were therefore obliged to restrict our experiment to larvae derived from eggs laid on cuckoo flower in fenland only. Rearing the insect in captivity on the three different foods presented no problems. The mortality during the first 8-10 days of larval life was considerable, but thereafter it dropped to negligible proportions. The results obtained from two batches of eggs are summarized in Table 27.

While the number of deaths in the two batches fed on *Cardamine* and *Alliaria* was of the same general order (20–30 per cent), that among *Tropaeolum* feeders was roughly three times greater in the first batch and about double in the second. It was not possible to establish the causes of failure with any precision but many larvae died about the time of the first ecdysis. The time of pupation and the duration of the pupal period seemed to be unrelated to the food of the larvae, while the mortality of pupae was of the order of 40 per cent and showed no variation with larval food.

Table 27 Mortality of green-veined white larvae on three different food plants.

Date hatched	Food plant	No. of larvae hatched	No. of larvae 23.v.60	% mortality
13.v.60	*Cardamine*	25	17	32.0
	Alliaria	25	20	20.0
	Tropaeolum	25	3	88.0
15.v.60	*Cardamine*	14	10	28.6
	Alliaria	14	10	28.6
	Tropaeolum	17	8	52.9

Throughout their period of growth the different batches of larvae were weighed each day in groups of 10. Some typical results covering the last five days of growth are shown in Fig. 29. Variation in food appeared to make comparatively little difference to the overall rate of development of the larvae, judged by increase in weight. However, the *pattern* of development in those fed on *Tropaeolum* differed markedly from that of the others living on *Cardamine* and *Alliaria*. Such divergence could certainly not have been predicted from the behaviour of the larvae. The food in all the cages was replenished daily and at no time was there any apparent reluctance to feed on the plant provided.

This experiment was little more than a trial run; a more extensive investigation using larger numbers of larvae would have been

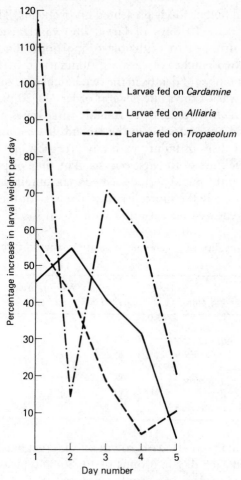

Figure 29 Variation in the pattern of development of green-veined white larvae reared on three different food plants.

necessary for any firm conclusions to be drawn. However, it indicates clearly the kind of results that might be expected and which could be of considerable significance. When discussing the life cycle of the meadow brown in Chapter 1, the point was made that the larvae undergo a marked change in feeding habits, being diurnal when small in the pre-hibernation period up to November, but nocturnal from late April onwards when they are larger. No doubt the altered behaviour serves to minimize the predation by birds that would otherwise occur. Any pattern of feeding that tended to upset this balance would be disadvantageous and therefore non-adaptive. This is a field of enquiry where little is known at present and which could yield significant information with a minimum outlay of resources.

In the previous pages I have attempted to describe a series of ecological problems, how they evolved one from another and how we attempted to solve them. No sooner had we found a partial answer to one of them than others arose. Some of the problems that faced us thirty years ago still remain, but today we can ask much more sophisticated questions about them as our background information and the experimental techniques at our disposal have developed. But in spite of these advances the basic ingredients of experimentation remain—asking the right questions, an intimate acquaitance with the experimental material, and rigorous observation and analysis. Throughout this book I have sought to show how we have tried to apply these approaches in the context of the meadow brown and the extent to which that work has contributed to the advance of knowledge, both of the life of the butterfly itself and of the principles underlying its ecology.

References

1. Lane, C. (1961) A note on the behaviour of the meadow brown (*Maniola jurtina*) (Lep. Satyridae) in Austria. *The Entomologists' Monthly Magazine*, **97**, 220.
2. Lane, C. and Rothschild, M. (1962) A note on the behaviour of the meadow brown (*Maniola jurtina*) (Lep. Satyridae) in Spain. *The Entomologists' Monthly Magazine*, **98**, 170.
3. Ford, E. B. (1962, 3rd edn) *Butterflies*. The New Naturalist Series, Collins, London.
4. Stokoe, W. J. (1944) *The Caterpillars of the British Butterflies*. Frederick Warne, London.
5. Dowdeswell, W. H. and McWhirter, K. (1967) Stability of spot-distribution in *Maniola jurtina* throughout its range. *Heredity*, **22**, 187–210.
6. Thomson, G. (1976) Le genre *Maniola* Schrank (Lepidoptera: Satyridae). Notes sur les génetalia mâles et femelles. *Linneana Belgica*, **6**, 126–42.
7. Ford, H. D. and Ford, E. B. (1930) Fluctuation in numbers and its influence on variation in *Melitaea aurinia*. *Transactions of the Entomological Society of London*, **78**, 345–51.
8. Dowdeswell, W. H. (1938) Further notes on the Lepidoptera of Cara Island. *Entomologist*, **70**, 1–7.
9. Dowdeswell, W. H., Fisher, R. A., and Ford, E. B. (1949) The quantitative study of populations in the Lepidoptera—1. *Polyommatus icarus* Rott. *Annals of Eugenics*, **10**, 123–36.
10. Fisher, R. A. and Ford, E. B. (1947) The spread of a gene in natural conditions in a colony of the moth *Panaxia dominula* L. *Heredity*, **1**, 143–74.
11. Dowdeswell, W. H. Fisher, R. A., and Ford, E. B. (1949) The quan-

titative study of the Lepidoptera—2. *Maniola jurtina* L. *Heredity*, **3**, 67–84.

12. Dowdeswell, W. H. and Ford, E. B. (1947) Butterfly migrations noted in the Isles of Scilly in 1947. *Entomologist*, **81**, 141.

13. Dowdeswell, W. H. and Ford, E. B. (1952) The distribution of spot-numbers as an index of geographical variation in the butterfly *Maniola jurtina* L (Lepidoptera: Satyridae). *Heredity*, **6**, 99–109.

14. Dowdeswell, W. H. and Ford, E. B. (1953) The influence of isolation on variability in the butterfly, *Maniola jurtina* L. *Symposia of the Society of Experimental Biology*, **7**, 254–73.

15. Dowdeswell, W. H. (1956) Isolation and adaptation in populations of the Lepidoptera. *Proceedings of the Royal Society* B, **145**, 322–9.

16. Creed, E. R., Dowdeswell, W. H., Ford, E. B., and McWhirter, K. G. (1959) Evolutionary studies on *Maniola jurtina*: the English Mainland, 1956–57. *Heredity*, **13**, 363–91.

17. Creed, E. R., Dowdeswell, W. H., Ford, E. B., and McWhirter, K. G. (1962) Evolutionary studies on *Maniola jurtina*: the English Mainland, 1958–60. *Heredity*, **17**, 237–65.

18. Foreman, B., Ford, E. B., and McWhirter, K. G. (1959) An evolutionary study of the butterfly *Maniola jurtina* in the north of Scotland. *Heredity* **13**, 353–61.

19. Brakefield, P. M. (1979) An experimental study of the maintenance of variation in spot-pattern in *Maniola jurtina*. *Ph.D. Thesis, Liverpool University*.

20. Creed, R. (ed.) (1971) *Ecological Genetics and Evolution: Essays in Honour of E. B. Ford*. Blackwell, Oxford.

21. McWhirter, K. G. and Creed, E. R. (1971) An analysis of spot-placing in the meadow brown butterfly, *Maniola jurtina*. In *Ecological Genetics and Evolution* (ed. Creed). Blackwell, Oxford.

22. Ford, E. B. (1975, 4th edn) *Ecological Genetics*. Chapman and Hall, London.

23. Dowdeswell, W. H. and McWhirter, K. (1967) Stability of spot-distribution in *Maniola jurtina* throughout its range. *Heredity*, **22**, 187–210.

24. Scali, V. (1971) Spot-distribution in *Maniola jurtina* (L) (Lepidoptera: Satyridae): Tuscan Mainland 1967–69. *Monitore Zool. Ital.*, **5**, 147–63.

25. Masetti, M. and Scali, V. (1972) Ecological adjustments of the reproductive biology in *Maniola jurtina* from Tuscany. *Accademia Nazionale Dei Lincei*, **53**, 460–8.

26. Scali, V. (1972) Spot-distribution in *Maniola jurtina*: Tuscan Archipelago, 1968–70. *Heredity*, **29**, 25–36.

27. Scali, V. (1971) Imaginal diapause and gonadal maturation of *Man-*

iola jurtina (Lepiodoptera: Satyridae) from Tuscany. *Journal of Animal Ecology*, **40**, 467-72.

28. Scali, V. and Masetti, M. (1973) The population structure of *Maniola jurtina* (Lepidoptera: Satyridae): the sex-ratio control. *Journal of Animal Ecology*, **42**, 773-8.

29. Darwin, C. (1859) *The Origin of Species*, Sixth Edition, reprinted 1956. The World's Classics series. Oxford University Press, Oxford.

30. Lack, D. (1947) *Darwin's Finches*. Cambridge University Press, Cambridge.

31. Dowdeswell, W. H., Ford, E. B., and McWhirter, K. G. (1960) Further studies on the evolution of *Maniola jurtina* in the Isles of Scilly. *Heredity*, **14**, 333-64.

32. Creed, E. R., Ford, E. B., and McWhirter, K. G. (1964) Evolutionary studies on *Maniola jurtina*: the Isles of Scilly, 1958-59. *Heredity*, **19**, 471-88.

33. Mayr, E. (1954) Change of genetic environment and evolution. In *Evolution as a Process*, eds Huxley, Hardy, and Ford. Allen and Unwin, London.

34. Waddington, C. H. (1957) *The Strategy of the Genes*. Allen and Unwin, London.

35. Dowdeswell, W. H. and Ford, E. B. (1955) Ecological genetics of *Maniola jurtina* on the Isles of Scilly. *Heredity*, **9**, 265-72.

36. Dowdeswell, W. H., Ford, E. B., and McWhirter, K. G. (1957) Further studies on isolation in the butterfly, *Maniola jurtina* L. *Heredity*, **11**, 51-65.

37. Shorrocks, B. (1978) *The Genesis of Diversity*. Hodder and Stoughton, London.

38. Dowdeswell, W. H. (1961) Experimental studies on natural selection in the butterfly, *Maniola jurtina*. *Heredity*, **16**, 39-52.

39. Dowdeswell, W. H. (1962) A further study of the butterfly, *Maniola jurtina* in relation to natural selection by *Apanteles tetricus*. *Heredity*, **17**, 513-23.

40. Dowdeswell, W. H. (1965), Studies of sympatric evolution in the meadow brown butterfly, *Maniola jurtina*. In *Scientific Research in Schools*. The Association for Science Education, Hatfield, Herts.

41. McWhirter, K. and Scali, V. (1966) Ecological bacteriology of the meadow brown butterfly. *Heredity*, **21**, 517-21.

42. Handford, P. T. (1973) Patterns of variation in a number of genetic systems in *Maniola jurtina*: the boundary region. *Proceedings of the Royal Society of London* B, **183**, 265-84.

43. Handford, P. T. (1973) Patterns of variation in a number of genetic systems in *Maniola jurtina*: the Isles of Scilly. *Proceedings of the Royal Society of London* B, **183**, 285-300.

44. Masetti, M. and Scali, V. (1975) Electrophoretic studies on gene-enzyme systems in *Maniola jurtina* (Lepidoptera: Satyridae): the PGM polymorphism in Central Italy. *Accademia Nazionale Dei Lincei*, **59**, 822-30.

45. Scali, V. and Masetti, M. (1980) Zygotic and fertility selection for phosphoglucomutase variants in natural populations of *Maniola jurtina* (Lepidoptera: Satyridae). *Accademia Nazionale Dei Lincei*, **67**, 137-44.

46. Masetti, M. and Scali, V. (1978) Distributione degli allozimi PGM nell'areale del Lepidottero *Maniola jurtina* L. *Associaone Genetica Italiana*, **23**, 177-9 and personal communication.

47. McWhirter, K. (1969) Heritability of spot-number in Scillonian strains of the meadow brown butterfly (*Maniola jurtina*). *Heredity*, **24**, 314-18.

48. Brakefield, P. M. (1977) Field studies on the meadow brown butterfly. *British Association for the Advancement of Science, Section D*.

49. Kettlewell, H. B. D. (1961) The phenomenon of industrial melanism in the Lepidoptera. *Annual Review of Entomology*, **6**, 246-62.

50. Thomson, G. (1971) The Manx race of *Maniola jurtina* (L) (Lep. Satyridae). *Entomologist's Record*, **83**, 91-4.

51. Ford, E. B. and Dowdeswell, W. H. (1948) The genetics of habit in the genus *Colias*. *Entomologist*, **81**, 209-12.

52. Dowdeswell, W. H. and Willcox, H. N. A. (1961) Influence of the food plant on growth rate and pre-imaginal mortality in the green-veined white butterfly, *Pieris napi* L. *Entomologist*, **94**, 2-8.

Index

ABERDEEN UNIVERSITY, 66
Aceto-orcein, stain for chromatin, 90
Adaptation, 20
Adaptive change, 2
Aestivation, 86-8
Aglais urticae, see small tortoiseshell
Agricultural practice, 145, 146
Alliaria petiolata, see garlic mustard
Androconia, *see* scent-producing scales
Annual meadow grass, 10
Anthocharis cardamines, see orange-tip
Apamea monoglypha, see dark arches moth
Apanteles tetricus (ichneumon), 123, 124, 126-7, 128, 144
Apanteles tibialis (ichneumon), 128
Aphantopus hyperanthus, see ringlet
Aposematic (warning) devices, 151
Archaeology, 42
Atlantic, migration across, 37
Austria, meadow brown in, 7

BACTERIAL INFESTATION, 123, 135
Barriers, ecological, 119
Beak marks, on butterfly wings, 138
Beaufoy, S., 59, 61, 62, 72
Behaviour patterns, 7, 8, 9, 118, 137, 149-51
Bimodality, of spotting, 44, 51, 60, 61
Binomial system of nomenclature, 2
Birdsfoot trefoil, 114

Biston betularia, see peppered moth
Black death, of larvae, 144
Black hairstreak, 16
Bodmin moor, as an ecological barrier, 47-8, 61
Boundary phenomenon, 50-9, 61, 64, 76, 125, 131, 135, 143
Brachypodium sylvaticum, see slender false-brome
Brakefield, P. M., 66-8, 127, 136-40, 144, 149, 152
Bramble, 6
British Museum (Natural History), 2, 80, 88
Buckley (Wales), meadow brown population, 128
Burham Down (Kent), meadow brown population, 70

CARA ISLAND (SCOTLAND), dark arches moth population, 22-5, 45
Cardamine pratensis, see cuckoo flower
Carpobrotus edulis, see hottentot fig
Cattle, as selective agents, 105-7, 144
Cellulose paint, for marking butterflies, 24, 27
Centaurea nigra, see knapweed
Central transect, 61-2
Cheesefoot Head (Hampshire), meadow brown population, 125-8, 129

Chi-squared (χ^2) test, 22
Classification, 13
Clifton, M. P., 80
Climatic change, influence of, 59
Cline, gradient of variation, 45, 53, 54, 149
Clouded yellow, 136, 149, 150-1
Coenonympha tullia, see large heath
Colias croceus, see clouded yellow
Colias eurytheme, see North American clouded yellow
Common blue, 26-9, 114, 148, 149
Copulation, in meadow brown, 9
Costality index, 74-7
Courtship, 118
Cramond Island (Scotland), meadow brown population, 128
Creed, E. R., 50, 53, 74
Cryptic (concealing) devices, 151
Cuckoo flower, 152
Cyprus, meadow brown in, 16

Danus plexippus, see milkweed
Dark ages, human populations, 42
Dark arches moth, 23-5
Darlow, H. M., 126
Dartmoor, as an ecological barrier, 47-8, 50, 61
Darwin, C., 43, 93
Density, of populations, 35
Development, pattern of, 152-5
Diapause, 86-8
Distribution, of meadow brown, 2
Dobzhansky, T., 59
Downy oat, 121

ECOLOGICAL BACTERIOLOGY, 128-9
barriers, 21, 105, 108, 143
genetics, 2, 42
isolation, 61
Ecology, study of, 2, 22
Electrophoresis, acrylamide-gel, 129
starch-gel, 132
Emigration, 21, 28, 35
Enzyme analysis, 131
variants, 132
Enzymes in meadow brown, 129, 130
Esterase, in meadow brown, 131

Euphydryas aurinia, see marsh fritillary
Europe, meadow brown in, 13, 78-92
Evolution of spot-stabilizations, 2, 101-11
Experimental populations, establishment of, 113-16

FELT-TIPPED PENS, for marking butterflies, 24, 27
Feock (Cornwall), meadow brown population, 44
Fisher, R. A., 24
Flat-topped spot-distribution, 97
Fluctuation in numbers, 104, 111
Ford, E. B., 8, 13, 20, 21, 36, 38, 42, 51, 66, 74, 76, 103, 104, 113, 136, 148, 150
Ford, H. D., 20, 104
Foreman, B., 66
Founder principle, 104, 111, 112-13
Frazer, J. D. F., 69

GALAPAGOS ISLANDS, finches of, 43, 93
Garlic mustard, 152
Genetic discontinuity, 57, 59
drift, 103-4, 105, 112-13
Genital structure, 134
Geography, of meadow brown, 13
Gigha Island (Scotland), 22, 23
Grampian mountains, 67
Gram stain, for bacteria, 128
Grayling, 148
Great Ganilly (Isles of Scilly), meadow brown populations, 105, 110-11, 131-2
Great Innisvowles (Isles of Scilly), meadow brown populations, 114-16
Great Orme's Head, butterfly populations on, 148
Green-veined white, 152

HANDFORD, P. T., 129, 131-4
Hayle (Cornwall), common blue population, 29
Hedge brown, 13, 148, 149, 152
Helictotrichon pubuscens, see downy oat

Herbicides, effects of, 145
Heritability of spotting, 136, 144
Heterogeneity, assessment of, 22
Hibernation, 11
Hightown (Liverpool), meadow brown population, 137
Hipparchia semele, see grayling
Homogeneity, assessment of, 22
Hottentot fig, 96, 98
Howarth, T. G., 80

IBERIAN PENINSULA, meadow brown populations, 143
Immigration, 21, 28, 35
Industrial melanism, 145, 146
Intermittent drift, 104, 111
Intra-seasonal shift, *see also* spot-variation, intra-seasonal, 70, 72, 88, 120
Ireland, meadow brown in, 18, 65
Iron age, human populations, 42
Isles of Scilly, large islands, 95–101
    meadow brown in, 93–116
    small islands, 101–11
Isolation, influence of, 21, 36
Italy, meadow brown in, 7, 84–92, 132

JARDINE, SIR W., 3

KETTLEWELL, H. B. D., 144, 145
Knapweed, 6, 145

LACK, D., 93
Land's End Peninsula, meadow brown populations, 48, 61
Lane, C., 7
Large heath, 149
    white, 151
Larval feeding (high/low), 124–5
    mortality, 126
    survival, 123
Life cycle of meadow brown, 8, 120, 154
Linnaeus, K., 1, 6
Lotus corniculatus, see birdsfoot trefoil
Lucerne, 151
Lycaena phlaeas, see small copper
Lycaenidae, 16

MACROCLIMATE, in grass tufts, 121
Maniola cypricola, 16, 84
Maniola jurtina, Manx dwarf form, 147
    sub-species *cassiteridum*, 18
    sub-species *iernes*, 18
    sub-species *splendida*, 18
Maniola nurag, see Sardinian meadow brown
Maniola telmessia, 16, 84, 143
Marbled white, 13
Marking butterflies, 24, 27
Marsh fritillary, 16, 20, 104, 148
Masetti, M., 132–5
Mayr, E., 59, 104
McWhirter, K. G., 50, 51, 66, 74, 78, 128, 135
Medicago sativa, see lucerne
Melanargia galathea, see marbled white
Melanic forms, 144
Melanin pigment, 145
Menawethan (Isles of Scilly), meadow brown population, 114–16
Microbiological Research Establishment (Porton), 126
Microclimate, in grass tufts, 121
Middleton (Hampshire), meadow brown population, 119–25, 128, 129, 134
Migration, 36, 101–3, 113
Milkweed, 37
Molinia caerulea, see purple moor grass
Move lengths (ML), distance travelled, 138

NASTURTIUM, 152
Nature Conservancy, 69
North American clouded yellow, 180–1
Nymphalidae, 16

OCELLUS, eye-spot, 3
Onobrychis viciifolia, see sainfoin
Orange-tip, 148
Oxford University, 66, 130

PAINTED LADY, 16
Pararge aegeria, see speckled wood
Penwith Peninsula, meadow brown on, 48, 57
Peppered moth, 144, 145
Phosphoglucomutase (PGM), enzyme in meadow brown, 132–5
Pieris brassicae, see large white
Pieris napi, see green-veined white
Pieris rapae, see small white
Plebejus argus, see silver-studded blue
Poa annua, see annual meadow grass
Poa pratensis, see smooth meadow grass
Pollution, industrial, 144, 146
Polyommatus icarus, see common blue
Population numbers, estimation of, 23–4, 27, 30–2, 104, 105, 112, 119, 137, 147
Post-aestivation, 88, 132
Pre-aestivation, 88
Probability, 22
Pseudomonas fluorescens (bacterium), as pathogen, 126
Pupal mortality, 123
Purple moor grass, 10
Pyronia tithonus, see hedge brown

RAGWORT, 116
Reverse cline, 54, 56, 57, 131
Ringlet, 13
Rothschild, M., 7
Rothschild, Second Baron, Walter, 80
Rubus fruticosus, see bramble

SAINFOIN, 151
St Andrews (Scotland), meadow brown population, 67
St Helen's (Isles of Scilly), meadow brown population, 104
St Martin's (Isles of Scilly), meadow brown population, 97–101, 114, 128, 131
St Mary's (Isles of Scilly), meadow brown population, 95–6
St Thiona and Tean, Isles of Scilly, 42
Sampling, problems of, 27, 30
Sardinian meadow brown, 13, 16

Satyridae, 11, 13, 84
Scali, V., 82, 88, 128, 132–5
Scent-producing scales, 3, 8, 13
Scoring of spot-values, 38
Scotland, meadow brown in, 18, 65–8
Selection, endocyclic, 92
  pressures, 104, 113
  visual, 139
Selective agents, 118–19
  elimination, 125
Senecio jacobaea, see ragwort
Sex chromatin, 90
  determination of, 90
  ratio, 89–92
Shorrocks, B., 111
Sidlaw Hills, meadow brown population, 67
Significance, statistical, 22
Silver-studded blue, 148
Sledge net, for larvae, 121
Slender false-brome, 121
Small copper, 116
Small tortoiseshell, 151
Small white, 37, 151
Smooth meadow grass, 10
Southern transect, 61–5
Spain, meadow brown in, 7
Speckled wood, 13
Spermatophore, 9
Spot-average, 54, 72
  -distribution, stability of, 72, 142
  -number, 72
  -placing, 72–7
  -size, 72
  -stabilization, east Cornish (EC), 46–72, 125, 131
    general European (GE), 80–1
    new English (NE), 51, 69
    old English (OE), 69
    peripheral populations, 81–2
    pseudo-Cornish (PC), 69
    southern English (SE), 45–72, 119, 125, 131, 143
    west Asian (WA), 84, 143
    west Cornish (WC), 50
Spotting, as a parameter of variation, 37–9
  inheritance of, 135–6

Spot-variation, inter-seasonal, 70
  intra-seasonal, 70, 126
Statistical methods, 22
Strymonidia pruni, see black hairstreak
Survival, in meadow brown adults, 35
  rates, 30, 137
Sweep net, for larvae, 121
Sympatry, 143
Synthetic flowers, 120

TAXONOMY (classification), 2
Tean (Isles of Scilly), common blue
  populations, 25-9
  meadow brown populations, 32-9,
    43, 104, 105-7, 144
Thomson, G., 134, 147
Ticket punch, for marking insects, 24
Tiverton (Devon), common blue in, 29
Tresco (Isles of Scilly), meadow brown
  populations, 96-7, 131
  Farm Area, 111-13
Tropaeolum sp., *see* nasturtium
Tuscany, meadow brown in, 84-92

Type specimens, 80

UNIMODALITY OF SPOTTING, 45, 60, 61
Uninhabited islands, living on, 40-2
University of Pisa, 82

Vanessa cardui, see painted lady
Vanessidae, 16
Variation (variability), 2, 22, 24, 28-9,
    147-55
  first-order, 68-72, 142
  geography of, 82-4
  index, in the common blue, 29
  inter-seasonal, 69, 72, 80
  intra-seasonal, 69-72
  second-order, 51, 59, 68-72, 97, 142

WADDINGTON, C. H., 105
White Island (Isles of Scilly) meadow
  brown on, 105, 107-9, 131-2
Willcox, H. N. A., 152
Winchester (Hampshire), meadow
  brown populations, 125, 134, 135